RELIGION IN CHINA

RELIGION IN CHINA

Survival and Revival under Communist Rule

FENGGANG YANG

郁丹之
指正！

杨凤岗

2014.6.5. 寄廷枢

OXFORD
UNIVERSITY PRESS

OXFORD
UNIVERSITY PRESS

Oxford University Press, Inc., publishes works that further
Oxford University's objective of excellence
in research, scholarship, and education.

Oxford   New York
Auckland   Cape Town   Dar es Salaam   Hong Kong   Karachi
Kuala Lumpur   Madrid   Melbourne   Mexico City   Nairobi
New Delhi   Shanghai   Taipei   Toronto

With offices in
Argentina   Austria   Brazil   Chile   Czech Republic   France   Greece
Guatemala   Hungary   Italy   Japan   Poland   Portugal   Singapore
South Korea   Switzerland   Thailand   Turkey   Ukraine   Vietnam

Copyright © 2012 by Oxford University Press, Inc.

Published by Oxford University Press, Inc.
198 Madison Avenue, New York, New York 10016

www.oup.com

Oxford is a registered trademark of Oxford University Press

Library of Congress Cataloging-in-Publication Data
Yang, Fenggang.
Religion in China : survival and revival under communist rule / Fenggang Yang.
    p. cm.
ISBN 978-0-19-973564-8
ISBN 978-0-19-973565-5
1. China—Religion—20th century.   2. Communism and religion—China—
History—20th century.   3. China—Religion—21st century.   4. Communism
and religion—China—History—21st century.   I. Title.
BL1803.Y34 2011
200.951'09045—dc22   2011010628

1 3 5 7 9 8 6 4 2

Printed in the United States of America
on acid-free paper

This book is dedicated to my father,
Yang Liansheng (1924–2009),
a lifelong Chinese Communist Party member
who was baptized into Christ on his deathbed upon
his request

PREFACE

This book has taken about a decade to complete from its initial conception to its current form. I began to conduct systematic empirical research on religion in China in 2000. The original plan was focusing on Christian ethics in the market transition, a project that draws theoretical reference from Max Weber,[1] one of the founding fathers of sociology. If the Protestant ethic, as Weber argues, was conducive to the emergence of modern capitalism in the West, would there be some Chinese Protestant ethic, and would it be conducive to the transition toward a market economy in China? However, during the process of collecting fieldwork and interview data in eight cities throughout China, I was frequently puzzled by various religious phenomena burning for understanding and explanation. To sum it up in one large question: How could religion survive and revive in China under Communist rule? Without answering this prime question first, I felt it impossible to move further to examine religion as a causal factor or an independent variable in the process of social change within contemporary China.

THE PREPARATION

To tackle this basic question about religion in China is not an easy undertaking for a person like myself, who was born and raised in China when religion was very much absent from the schools and the larger society. At school, if there was anything we learned about religion, it was that religion was the opium of the people; only the oppressed and the weak would resort to superstitious religious beliefs. In the rural community in northern China where I grew up, religion was not part of village life. The only remotely religious things in my childhood that I can now recall are a few ghost stories told by the old villagers during long, dark, and boring nights and an occasion of Daoist ritualists performing at a funeral. Upon hearing such stories or seeing such rituals, people, at least my peers, would simply laugh them off. We were taught at school that we must establish a scientific outlook on life (*jianli kexue de rensheng guan*); it was believed that only science and technology and Mao Zedong Thought would make society progress toward the future beautiful Communist Society.

My personal experience of growing up in China is not an exception. An American visitor observed during his trip to China in 1972: "During our visit we saw almost no evidence of surviving religious practice.... We saw no functioning Buddhist temples. Some of those we visited had been converted to use as tea houses, hostels or assembly halls; others were maintained as museums.... Some Chinese with whom we talked were curious about religion. They were amazed to learn that educated persons in the West continue to believe and practice religion. For them, they said, the study of scientific materialism had exposed the logical fallacies and absurdities of religion."[2]

From kindergarten to college, the absence of religion in school lasted well into the 1980s. Many years after that, religion was still absent in most communities, even though, beginning in 1979, a limited number of temples, churches, and mosques were allowed to reopen for religious services. Moreover, even if there was a church or temple in a neighborhood, most of the local residents might not be aware of its presence. During my 2000 field research in several cities in China, I asked several times for directions to a nearby church or temple, but people in the street simply had no clue that there was a church or temple in the neighborhood, even though the church or temple was within a hundred meters from where we were standing.

After entering graduate school in 1984, while studying Western philosophy, somehow I became fascinated with Hegel's Absolute Spirit, Kant's ideal of pure reason and postulate of practical reason, and the concepts of God and religion in general. In my master's thesis, "On the Evolution of the Notion of God in Western Philosophy,"[3] I examined the arguments by major philosophers from ancient Greece until modern times. After receiving my master's degree in Western philosophy, I took a job in religious studies in the philosophy department of Renmin University of China in Beijing. That was in 1987, when both religion and the study of religion were recovering from elimination during the Cultural Revolution (1966–1976). To my surprise, in the "Introduction to the Study of Religion" (*Zongjiao Xue Gailun*) course, which I taught for a semester, about 120 students from various departments were enrolled. Besides the curious and enthusiastic students, I also encountered devout believers at tourist or religious sites. Such phenomena of living religion eventually led me to pursue a doctorate in the sociology of religion.

Through a series of fortuitous opportunities, or by divine providence, as one may say, I arrived at the Catholic University of America in Washington, D.C., in early 1989 and in fall began my PhD studies under the guidance of the well-known sociologist of religion Dean R. Hoge.[4] After the Chinese Communist authorities sent tanks into Tiananmen Square and crushed the democracy movement in 1989, many Chinese students and scholars studying in the United States began to flock to Christian churches. Actually, in both China and North America, large numbers of Chinese began actively searching and turning to Christianity for the meaning of life and the future of the Chinese nation. I have been drawn to this unprecedented cultural and social phenomenon of mass conversion to Christianity in the history of China and Chinese America and have conducted a number of empirical studies of it.[5] I have also studied various immigrant religions in the United States.[6] Since 2002, I have been teaching "Religion in America" to Purdue undergraduates on a regular basis. Through all of these learning and research experiences, I have gained knowledge regarding both the various religions and the sociological theories of religion, which has prepared me to tackle the basic and general questions of religion in China.

THE SCOPE AND ORGANIZATION OF THIS BOOK

The rapid social changes in Chinese society have attracted many scholars to conduct original research, but until recently, religious change has been very much neglected by social scientists both inside and outside China. This negligence may have historical and intellectual reasons. Since the May Fourth and New Culture movements around 1919, Chinese elite intellectuals, influenced by European Enlightenment discourses, have become critical of and despising toward religion. The received wisdom has been that the Chinese as a whole have never been religious. Hu Shih, one of the most influential Chinese intellectuals in the twentieth century, states, "China is a country without religion and the Chinese are a people who are not bound by religious superstitions."[7] Many Chinese scholars and Western sinologists share this view.[8] However, this is a problem of the armchair philosophers and theologians who read texts instead of observing human beings. Anthropologists and sociologists who have been there and done observations report a totally different reality. Fifty years ago, the Chinese-born American sociologist C. K. Yang published *Religion in Chinese Society*, which argues effectively with empirical evidence that until the Communist Revolution, religion was very much diffused in all social institutions. "There was not one corner in the vast land of China [before 1949] where one did not find temples, shrines, altars, and other places of worship [which] were a visible indication of the strong and pervasive influence of religion in Chinese society."[9]

What has happened to religion since the Communist Revolution? Since the work of C. K. Yang, there have been some sinological and anthropological studies of religious rituals and local communities that have shed light on some aspects of the religious life in contemporary Chinese society. However, no publication has described and explained the overall religious landscape or the macro process of religious change within Chinese society. The exceptional few sociological studies of contemporary religion focus on one particular religion in Chinese society.[10] With this book, I attempt to present a comprehensive overview of the religious change under the Chinese Communists and suggest a theoretical explanation for it.

The immense diversity of religion and regional variations within China deserve to be documented and analyzed with numerous volumes of books. However, we have to struggle to stay above water without drowning in the countless details in the attempt to present a bird's-eye view. Throughout the book, I try to be parsimonious yet sufficient, two essential principles of the scientific enterprise.

To implement this project, here is the plan. Chapter 1 reviews the literature of the sociology of religion, discusses the shift from the secularization paradigm to the new paradigm of religious vitality, and proposes a political-economic approach to explain religion in China under Communist rule. Chapter 2 presents a definition of religion combined with a classification scheme, which is needed for the political-economic approach that examines religion and its competitive alternatives within the larger society. Chapter 3 examines the Chinese Communist understanding of atheism and its implications for the religious policy. Chapter 4 describes the historical evolution of the religious policy under Chinese Communist rule. Chapters 5 and 6 make up the theoretical core of the book, articulating the triple-religious-market model in a shortage economy of religion. In the concluding chapter 7, I argue that religion in China under Communist rule is only one case of religious oligopoly; that is, not a single one but a selected few religions are sanctioned by the state. Oligopoly is the most common type of religion-state relations in the world today. What we have learned by examining contemporary China may be applicable to or indicative of religious dynamics in other oligopoly societies under heavy regulation.

ACKNOWLEDGMENTS

THIS ENORMOUSLY CHALLENGING work would have been impossible without help from various institutions and numerous individuals, to whom I am very grateful. The initial financial support for my empirical research on religion in China came as small grants from Professional and Educational Services International, the University of Southern Maine Faculty Senate Research Fund, the Society for the Scientific Study of Religion Research Grant, the Religious Research Association Research Grant, the Purdue College of Liberal Arts Dean's Research Incentive Grant, and the Purdue Research Fund Summer Faculty Grant.

From 2004 to 2008, a couple of generous grants from the Henry Luce Foundation supported the annual Summer Institute for the Scientific Study of Religion in China, with participants from universities throughout China. Through the Summer Institutes, I have not only learned about various kinds of religious phenomena in China but have also received good feedback during the process of my theoretical development of the triple religious market model and the shortage economy of religion theory.

Since 2006, I have received several generous grants from the John Templeton Foundation, supporting an interview project in the Spiritual Capital Program to study "Faith and Trust in the Emerging Market Economy of China" and organizing the Beijing Summit on Chinese Spirituality and Society in 2008. The current Chinese Spirituality and Society Program supports the annual Summer Institute and provides research grants to scholars studying religion in China.

Throughout the last decade or so, I have had the good fortune to work with many fine scholars in China. They are too many to be listed here, but my theoretical thinking has especially benefited from exchanges with Gao Shining of the Chinese Academy of Social Sciences, Li Xiangping of East China Normal University, and Wei Dedong of Renmin University of China, who has been my longtime collaborator in organizing the annual Summer Institute. Meanwhile, many colleagues in America and Europe have offered constructive critiques of my ideas and writings in a span of many years. Again, the list of these people would be too long. However, I must acknowledge the very helpful comments received from Grace Davie, Roger Finke, Graeme Lang, Daniel Olson, and R. Stephen Warner. Lewis R. Rambo read through the manuscript and provided many helpful comments and suggestions. I am also grateful to editor Theo Calderara for his helpful suggestions, patience, and encouragement throughout the process. Of course, all of the remaining deficiencies of this book are mine alone.

This book integrates several of my previously published articles with important revision, expansion, and updates: "Between Secularist Ideology and Desecularizing Reality: The Birth and Growth of Religious Research in Communist China," *Sociology of Religion* 65, no. 2 (2004): 101–119; "The

Red, Black, and Gray Markets of Religion in China,"
Sociological Quarterly 47 (2006): 93–122; "Religion in China
under Communism: A Shortage Economy Explanation,"
Journal of Church and State 52, no. 1 (2010): 3–33; and
"Oligopoly Dynamics: Consequences of Religious Regulation," *Social Compass* 57 (2010): 194–205. The long processes
of reviews, rejections, responses, and revisions of these
journal articles tested and improved my theoretical arguments. Receiving the 2006 Distinguished Article Award from
the American Sociological Association Section of the
Sociology of Religion for the triple market article significantly boosted my confidence in the theoretical development.
All of these show that the sociology of religion is a collective
enterprise, even though the book bears my name as the
author.

Finally, I am indebted to my wife, Joanne, and my daugh-
ters, Connie and Minnie. Their love, patience, understanding,
and support have sustained me throughout these years.

CONTENTS

RELIGION IN CHINA

EXPLAINING RELIGIOUS VITALITY

IN CHINA, RELIGION has survived a brutal attempt at eradication during the so-called Cultural Revolution of 1966–1976. Since then, in spite of continuous Communist rule, many kinds of religions have been reviving and thriving. The Chinese Communist Party maintains an atheist ideology; continues to enforce atheist propaganda through the education system, mass media, and numerous party and state organs; and carries out frequent crackdowns on religious groups. Yet religion has been growing by leaps and bounds throughout the country since the late 1970s.

That religion can survive and thrive under atheist Communist rule raises important theoretical and practical questions. How much can the state control the growth or decline of religion? Specifically, why did eradication measures fail? To what extent can a secularist state promote secularization? If heavy regulation is not effective in reducing religious participation, what are the reasons and consequences? What theory may help us understand the resilience of religion in a society with one-fifth of the world's population?

For a long time, the dominant theory in the sociology of religion was secularization theory, which anticipates the decline, or the declining significance, of religion in modern societies. This theory is apparently of no value for understanding religious vitality in China. In fact, secularization theory has served as the theoretical justification for the Communist governments, in the name of social and political progress, to carry out political campaigns to eradicate religion. By the end of the twentieth century, it became evident that Communist eradication efforts had failed, as documented by an increasing number of scholars.[1] The irreligiousness of the masses under Communist rule was superficial, illusory, or temporary at best. In most of the post-Communist European societies, religion rebounded quickly after the collapse of the Soviet regimes. A rare exception is East Germany, where the rebound of religiosity in conventional religion has been modest. However, the deviant case or outlier cannot overturn the general pattern, although it is valuable to seek explanations.[2]

Against the general pattern of religious vitality, Chinese Communist officials and researchers have repeatedly denounced the "religious fevers" spreading in society. In their eyes, religious vitality is abnormal in the current social context. China has been undergoing rapid modernization under the leadership of the atheist Communist Party. Within its own logic, religion should decline in such a context, as predicted by secularization theory, be it Marxist or another kind. However, this is "abnormal" only because of the Communist officials' dogmatic mentality, because they cannot think unless it is in terms of secularization theory. But to seek the truth in facts (*shi shi qiu shi*), as a mantra of the reform-era Chinese Communists goes, one needs first to acknowledge the facts before seeking a theoretical explanation. The obvious fact of religious change in China is not decline but resilience. Then, to explain this obvious fact, we have to seek a suitable theory. Secularization theory does not provide the kind of conceptual tools proper for the task in front of us. In spite of variably nuanced recent articulations and cautious qualifications, secularization nonetheless remains a theory of religious decline. It would be simply inept to apply it to explain the facts of religious survival and revival in China under Communist rule.

In the 1990s, a new paradigm in the sociology of religion arose to explain religious vitality in the United States and elsewhere. Among the various theories within the new paradigm, the market theory of religion or the so-called economics of religion appears to be the most promising approach to explain the macro-level of religious change in a society. To achieve a clearer understanding of religion in China under Communist rule, however, the set of concepts and propositions that have been developed largely by examining religious phenomena in America and Europe needs substantial improvement. My theoretical position is that adopting the scientific approach is seeking to explain general patterns amid variations and particularities; conversely, the empirical examination of variations and particularities should inform and improve the generalized concepts and propositions in the theoretical development.

THE PARADIGM SHIFT

Secularization is a social theory, a political ideology, and a sociological paradigm, all of which are entangled together. As a social theory, it predicts the inevitable decline of religious beliefs and/or the declining social significance of religion along with modernization. Following many modern thinkers, including the founding fathers of sociology,

Peter L. Berger in the 1960s articulated a refined version of secularization theory.[3] Religious pluralism, he argued, fractures the "sacred canopy" of a society. As people of multiple faiths come to interact in the modernized society, each faith system becomes inevitably relativized in their truth claims. Over time, more and more people would lose faith, and religion is destined to wither away. In 1968, Berger told the *New York Times* that by the twenty-first century, "religious believers are likely to be found only in small sects, huddled together to resist a worldwide secular culture."[4] This expressed the common view of intellectuals at that time. In North America and Europe, "God is dead" was pronounced by intellectuals, including some Christian theologians.[5] On the other side of the planet, Chinese Red Guards wiped out religious vestiges of the past backward times throughout China (at least, it seemed so on the surface).

Secularization theory served as the theoretical justification for the political ideology of secularization. As British sociologist of religion David Martin first suggested in the 1960s, "it was *in part* an ideological projection on history based on an apotheosis of reason, on an existentialist anticipation of autonomous man, and on a Marxist leap into freedom and into reality with the conclusion of the historical dialectic in class society."[6] With secularization as a political ideology, believers in secularization have mobilized state power and other resources to fight against religious beliefs and to drive religion out of political, educational, and other social institutions. This has happened in France, the United States, and many other Western societies. The ideological nature of secularization took a violent turn under the Communist regimes.

Both the social theory and the political ideology were fossilized and reinforced by the sociological paradigm of secularization. As Martin puts it, "certain assumptions taken together constitute a paradigm, and as Thomas Kuhn argued, we are extremely reluctant to alter that paradigm. Evidence may pile up against it, but we prefer to keep explaining *away* the evidence to altering the paradigm."[7] Martin very well summarizes the secularization paradigm: "what, then, of what used to be the undisputed paradigm of secularization? Sociology and modernity were born together and so the focus of sociology was on what happened to religion under conditions of modernity and accelerating change. Basically it characterized modernity as a scenario in which mankind shifted from the religious mode to the secular. Secularization was made part of a powerful social and historical narrative of what had once been and now was ceasing to be."[8] In other words, as a sociological paradigm, it frames macro-, meso-, and micro-level theories that treat religious decline or declining significance as the norm, against which it tries to explain away the so-called exceptional or temporary phenomena of religious persistence in modern societies. This paradigm began to erode in the 1960s through the 1980s. By the 1990s, it was effectively dismantled by an increasing number of sociologists of religion in the United States and elsewhere who were actually "seeking the truth in facts" through empirical studies.

The massive fact is that religion in the United States remained vibrant throughout the twentieth century and is still vibrant today. While mainline Protestant denominations have been losing members since the 1960s, evangelical and Pentecostal churches have been growing.[9] While some individuals have lost their faith and dropped out of church, others have returned to church, and still many more have switched denominations or converted to different faiths.[10]

There certainly have been religious changes but no clear sign of overall religious decline in this modernized society.[11] In fact, some scholars have shown that between the founding of the United States and the 1990s, when American society went through the modernization process, the proportion of religious adherents in the population increased.[12] Moreover, as José Casanova and many others have shown, religion continues to play significant roles both in American politics and in other parts of the modern world.[13]

Facing this empirical evidence of religious vitality within the United States, the secularization paradigm at first led some people to resort to American exceptionalism as an explanation. That is, the United States must be exceptional in going against the modern trend of all-encompassing secularization; it is only a matter of time before the United States begins to follow the norm of the modern world and see religious decline. However, dissatisfied with the secularization assumptions that go against the mounting empirical facts, an increasing number of American scholars began to develop alternative theories to explain the religious vitality in the United States. By the early 1990s, this innovative theorizing had reached such a level that R. Stephen Warner heralded the emerging new paradigm of the sociology of religion in the United States.[14] This new paradigm, in a nutshell, treats religious vitality in the United States as a normal state, although the theoretical explanations of the religious vitality by various scholars vary. Warner's conceptualization of the new paradigm stirred up intense debate.[15] By the early twenty-first century, the new paradigm has consolidated and prevailed,[16] even though a number of scholars continue to carry on the secularization debate. Indeed, some European scholars have continued vehemently rejecting the new paradigm, insisting on the inevitable decline of religion or its social significance in Europe and elsewhere.[17]

In response to the rejection by European scholars and in defense of the assertion of the new paradigm, Warner made a modest statement that the new paradigm as he originally described it would apply specifically and only to explain religion in the United States, whereas the secularization paradigm might be more suitable to explain religion in Europe. Following this logic, there would be other theoretical paradigms to explain religion in China and other parts of the world. Indeed, in an interview published by *China Ethnic News* on July 25, 2006, under the title "Hoping Chinese Scholars to Develop Theories and the Paradigm More Suitable to Explain Religion in China," R. Stephen Warner said that no paradigm in the sociology of religion could be applied to every society. Two years later, in another interview published by the same newspaper on September 19, 2008, entitled "Equality and Exchange: The Sociological Research of Religion in Contemporary Contexts," Warner reiterated that "the new paradigm is a way to understand American religion, which is different from European religion. Grace Davie has come along to say that many societies have in their own ways dealt with religion. I think that is terribly important. China also has its own way of dealing with religion." He then commented on my 2006 article "The Red, Black, and Gray Markets of Religion in China": "I would say his model is a Chinese paradigm. He is stimulated by rational choice thinking, but I don't think his model is best understood as an application of rational choice theory. It's an imagining and conceptualizing of the way religion works in China using different theoretical tools, one of which is the work of Finke and Stark." While I agree and appreciate his last comment on the fact that I have borrowed various theoretical tools in developing the triple religious market model, I cannot agree with him that the triple religious market model is a uniquely Chinese paradigm. In fact, the last section of my 2006 article especially points to the possible application of this model to medieval Europe, contemporary Latin America, and other societies. I articulate this point further in the last chapter of this book.

The seeming modesty of Warner's theoretical position of multiple paradigms for America, Europe, and China betrays the nature of science. On this matter, I share the view expressed by Rodney Stark and Roger Finke in their foreword to *Acts of Faith*, "To the Chinese Readers": "If it would be foolish to try to formulate a physics that only applies to the United States, or a biology that held only in Korea, it is equally foolish to settle for a sociology of religion that applies only to Western nations."[18] The scientific paradigm must be universally applicable, and the new one may replace the old one, just as in cosmology the old paradigm of the Ptolemaic system was replaced by the new paradigm of the Copernican system. Certainly, social sciences are human sciences that are different from physical sciences because the social-scientific research is on human behaviors, cultures, and societies. Working in a discipline of social science, sociologists of religion must recognize and appreciate religious variations among individuals, groups, communities, and societies. But the goal of science, including social science, as a modern enterprise, is to discover lawlike patterns across variations. This is an important characteristic of social science. It sets itself apart from certain disciplines of the humanities that seek to establish the idiosyncratic uniqueness of the particular events, cases, or people. Both humanities and social sciences are valuable pursuits of knowledge and understanding of the human life, but the distinctive characteristic of social science should not be relinquished. Of course, we must be cautious, must try hard not to overgeneralize or oversimplify patterns by ignoring substantive variations. As it happens, and as will be demonstrated in this book, when the level of generalization is properly devised, certain patterns may emerge among what have been previously perceived as mere variations.

Just like the scientific revolution in natural sciences, as it is presented by Thomas Kuhn,[19] the paradigm shift in the sociology of religion proves to be a painful process for some of the secularization advocates. In spite of the accumulated empirical evidence of a worldwide religious persistence or resurgence, which made even Peter Berger recant his own old theory of secularization,[20] some people cling to the thinking of exceptionalism. Now they propose that perhaps it is Western Europe that is the exceptional case. Some other scholars seem to be torn between the conflicting perceptions. Should the United States or Europe be regarded as the exceptional case?[21] Unsurprisingly, some people also argue for Chinese exceptionalism, asserting that Chinese religion and religiosity are so unique that no theory based on the studies of Europe or America is suitable to explain China.[22] This theoretical position is like throwing out the baby with the bath water. To the ears of such exceptionalists, Warner's words of parallel paradigms become almost musical. But such appeasement can only be a stumbling block for the scientific enterprise.

Actually, secularization theory may not necessarily hold true for Europe, either. Grace Davie reports that the majority of Europeans have not lost their religious beliefs, although their church attendance is much lower than that of Americans.

Davie describes the European religious situation as "believing without belonging."[23] With the support of such empirical evidence, the new paradigm theorists extend their theory to explain the religious situation in Europe.[24] According to Rodney Stark and others, the lower church attendance in Europe has nothing to do with advanced modernity or modernization; it is the result of religious regulations and the remnants of the state church in European societies. In a deregulated free market such as in the United States, religious pluralism and free competition are likely to lead to greater religious participation. This is not only true in the United States. Some empirical evidence has been used to explain how this could also happen in Europe.[25] An important issue needs to be noted here. There have been ongoing debates about the relationship between religious pluralism and religious vitality. While the negative correlation between religious pluralism and religious vitality has been rejected by most scholars, including Berger himself, the positive correlation between religious pluralism and religious participation has been subject to fierce dispute. This debate has involved painstaking technicalities of measurements and statistical procedures. However, the scholars of this debate have made little effort to clarify the concept of pluralism itself. I will address the related issues in chapter 7. Here I would like to stay focused on the new paradigm.

Without giving up the old paradigm or rejecting the new paradigm, Davie compares these paradigms to maps and insists that a map of the Rockies cannot be used to climb the Alps.[26] However, the map metaphor may not take us far down the road of the social-scientific study of religion. The new paradigm is not an end product of a map. Rather, it is more like a new set of map-making tools—cartography and topography. Whereas the maps of different landscapes will differ, the improved topographic and cartographic techniques will help to create more accurate and more useful maps. By now, the market theory of the new paradigm has been fruitfully applied to explain various religious landscapes in Latin America and post-Communist eastern Europe.[27] When it comes to the task of mapping out the religious landscape in China, it becomes clear that the new paradigm of religious vitality provides a more suitable, more proper, and categorically better set of theoretical tools than the secularization paradigm.

Furthermore, the Chinese religious landscape, because of the country's long history and because it has been under Communist rule for sixty years, certainly has many distinct characteristics. The existing cartography and topography that have been developed by studying Western landscapes may not be able to capture all of the distinct yet important characteristics of the Chinese landscape. Therefore, theoretical adaptations and improvements are necessary. On the other hand, if the topographical and cartographical techniques can be refined by examining the Chinese landscape, such improved tools may also become useful to improve the mapping of Western and other landscapes.

At this point, it does not seem necessary to continue with a refutation of the secularization theory, because this book is about religious resilience and vitality in China today. To those who want to dwell on excuses for holding on to the old paradigm that has been effectively dismantled or for clinging to one or the other exceptionalism, as Jesus once told such a man: "Let the dead bury their own dead" (Matthew 8: 22). Instead, I shall now align myself with the new paradigm of the sociology of religion and move forward by developing a political-economic approach. The political-economic approach starts with appropriating basic concepts in the existing economic approach but correcting its oversimplifications of the one-sided supply-side theorizing.

RELIGIOUS DEMAND, SUPPLY, AND REGULATION

The economic approach to the sociology of religion starts with the simple idea that religion consists of an economy much like commercial and other economies: "A religious economy consists of all of the religious activity going on in any society: a 'market' of current and potential adherents, a set of one or more organizations seeking to attract or maintain adherents, and the religious culture offered by the organization(s)."[28]

Like commercial economies, the religious economy is sensitive to changes in the market structure. The most significant market change is often regulation or deregulation: "Regulation restricts competition by changing the incentives and opportunities for religious producers (churches, preachers, revivalists, etc.) and the viable options for religious consumers (church members)."[29]

According to Stark and Finke, a religious monopoly, enforced by state regulation, breeds a lazy clergy and consequently a less religiously mobilized population. Conversely, in a deregulated market—that is, a free market—religious pluralism tends to prevail over monopoly: "To the degree that a religious economy is unregulated, it will tend to be very pluralistic," that is, there will be more religious "firms" competing for a share of the market.[30] Moreover, Proposition

75 in Stark and Finke's *Acts of Faith* states, "To the degree that religious economies are unregulated and competitive, overall levels of religious participation will be high."[31] This proposition needs to be refined and reformulated in light of oligopolistic dynamics, to which we will return later in this chapter and elaborate on in chapter 7.

Religious change in the United States appears to be strong evidence in favor of deregulation effects. In the more than 200 years since the First Amendment to the U.S. Constitution disestablished religion at the federal level, that is, deregulated the religious market, the rate of religious adherence in the U.S. population steadily increased from 17 percent in 1774 to 62 percent in 1980 and remains so in 2000, according to Finke and Stark.[32] In contrast, although religious freedom is written into the constitutions of most modern nation-states, western European countries, until recently, either maintained official state churches that were fully supported by universal religious taxes or favored particular churches with state subsidies and other privileges. According to Stark and associates, the lower rates of religious participation in some contemporary western European countries are, to a large extent, a consequence of religious establishment or its remnants.[33] Although this conclusion is subject to empirical verification or falsification, as some scholars have been trying to do by scrutinizing historical data in various societies, we do not need to dwell on it. Suffice it to say that the deregulation effect in the United States and some other countries is robust.

Obviously, regulation is a very important concept in economic theories of religion, but it needs clarification. Critics have rightly pointed out that there is no completely unregulated market and that state regulations can be either *against* religion or *for* religion.[34] Therefore, to delineate this concept further, it is necessary to distinguish the broad and narrow understandings of religious regulation. A broad definition may include all laws and rules enacted to govern religious affairs. In the United States, for example, the First Amendment establishes basic rules. Zoning, taxation, and other regulations are also pertinent to religious organizations. In this sense, there is no "unregulated" religious economy. No modern country "actually allows the unfettered exercise of that freedom,"[35] and "to allow completely unrestricted freedom would be socially unsound."[36] On the other hand, U.S. regulations are intended not to restrict any particular faith but to ensure equal competition and free religious exercise, although the reality may fall short of this ideal. Of course, the quintessence of regulation is restriction. Legal rules impose restrictions either on certain specific groups or on all groups regarding certain practices or operations. Therefore, regulation as restriction may serve as the narrow definition of religious regulation, as implied by Stark and other scholars.

Furthermore, restrictive regulation is a variable, ranging from highly restrictive to minimal across societies or in different periods within a society. Chaves and Cann suggested a six-item scale to quantify regulation of religious economies.[37] Alternatively, we may measure it on the ordinal level. At one extreme lies a complete ban or eradication of all religions. This is rarely practiced in human history and was short-lived, as evidenced by Albania[38] and China under the radical Communists. In the former Soviet Union and other Soviet societies, at least some religious groups existed legally throughout the period. Closest to the extreme of eradication is the monopoly, in which all but one religion are banned. Medieval Europe and some contemporary Muslim countries are quintessential monopoly economies, with a particular faith protected by the state through heavy regulation against "deviant" groups. Next to monopoly is oligopoly, in which several religions are sanctioned and all others are suppressed. Most present-day countries fall into this category, as will be further discussed in chapter 7. At the other extreme lies the so-called laissez-faire or free market, in which no religious group is singled out for restriction, although minimal administrative restrictions may be imposed on all. The United States is a free market par excellence.

It is important to note that in monopoly or oligopoly economies, regulation will not only ban other religions but will also impose certain restrictions on the favored faith or faiths. In exchange for political protection or privileges, the sanctioned religion(s) must accept political restrictions. The state may watch closely for deviance by the sanctioned religion(s). Similarly, a free market is not unregulated if we understand "regulation" in the broader sense.

Returning to Stark and Finke, Proposition 75 in *Acts of Faith* seems to imply that deregulation leads to increased religious participation. If this is so, a regime that desires to reduce religion will strive to maintain or increase religious regulation. The Chinese government under the Chinese Communist Party (CCP) is such a regime and has exactly done so in the last three decades. After abandoning the eradication policy, the CCP has been trying hard to regulate religion with increased measures and numbers of regulations. Contrary to its expectation, however, suppressive or restrictive regulation has not been effective. Religions have revived and are thriving despite heavy regulation.

On the surface, it appears true that in the more regulated markets of contemporary western Europe, participation in institutional religion is lower than in the less regulated U.S. market. On the other hand, there are more new religious movements (NRMs) in Europe than in the United States. The United States has 1.7 NRMs per million people, while Europe has 3.4 NRMs per million. This anomaly is more pronounced when considering that NRMs in Europe tend to be undercounted.[39] If this is close to reality, restrictive regulation evidently fails to reduce marginal or illegal NRMs. In fact, restrictive regulation is associated with a higher per-capita rate of NRMs. This seems ironic, but it points to an "invisible hand" of market forces in effect. Regarding this point, Stark and Finke fail to provide a formal proposition to complement Proposition 75. An improved theoretical model is required to explain the market forces that remain unaccounted for in their theory.

In the existing literature on the economic approach to the study of religion, the supply-side theory has been dominant, so much so that many people mistakenly equate the economic approach to the supply-side model.[40] The supply-side theorists assume that religious demand in a society is relatively stable and distributed in a bell-curve shape, in which the majority of people cluster in the middle niches while fewer people desire for either extremely high tension or extremely low tension with the surrounding culture. Individuals may change their religious preferences over time, but the normal distribution of religious demand in the whole population remains stable. If this is so, religious change is largely driven by supply-side shifts, including new religious "firms" (religious groups) entering the market or moving in or out of particular market niches.[41] However, in the "supply-side explanations," the stability of religious demand is assumed, not proven. This assumption may be needed in order to focus on the examination of supply-side dynamics. However, it is a mistake to take the assumption as a fact in all economies. Some scholars employing the economic approach have already pointed to the need to take "both demand and supply factors into account" to understand changes in religious market structures.[42]

The stable-demand assumption becomes simply implausible when examining religious change in China. As later chapters will show, when the religious supply was banned during the radical Cultural Revolution in the 1960s and 1970s, the active demand for religion was effectively reduced, although it was never reduced to zero, despite severe penalties to the steadfast believers. Arguably, it was the persistent demand, although at a reduced level, that eventually forced the Communist authorities to abandon the impossible mission of eradicating religion in the foreseeable future. Having adopted a relatively more pragmatic policy toward religion in 1979, the Communist authorities have nevertheless wished to contain religion and maintain a reduced level of religious participation in the population. The Party-state has imposed an increasing number of regulations to restrict the religious supply. However, the demand for religion appears to be continuously rising, surpassing the quotas of the supply set by the central and local governments and rendering the regulations on the supply side ineffective in many areas, as evidenced by the emergence of the "black" and "gray" markets of religion, which will be discussed in chapter 5 below.

In short, the Chinese case makes it necessary to make a focused examination of the demand-side changes rather than assuming its stability. To explain the interactions between demand and supply under heavy regulation, it becomes necessary to seek additional theoretical constructs beyond the existing economic approach of Stark and associates.

THE POLITICAL NATURE OF RELIGIOUS ECONOMIES

It is fair to recognize that the overwhelming attention to the supply side of the religious economy in the existing literature is not inadvertent. These researchers have primarily focused on the religious market of the United States, which has been a free market with minimal government interference and has become a saturated market wherein all demand niches have been very much occupied by numerous religious "firms." In such a chronic buyers' market, just as in the material-goods and housing economies, market change is commonly due to the result of changes arising on the supply side. If a religious firm shifts its religious goods to occupy different niches, this may determine its growth or decline because of the varied sizes of market niches in a plausible bell-curve normal distribution.[43]

But there exists another kind of market, the chronic sellers' market, wherein demand always exceeds supply. Indeed, shortage of supply is chronic and systemic in the "socialist system" under Communist rule, which is characterized by shortage in consumer goods, long queues in shops, long delays in services, and shortage throughout the production process. According to the renowned Hungarian and Harvard economist János Kornai, "The shortage phenomena under the classical socialist system are general, frequent, intensive, and chronic; the system is a shortage economy."[44] Many of Kornai's insights on the material economy in the "socialist countries" can be extended to the religious economy under Communist rule, as will be elaborated in chapter 6 below. The Chinese religious economy remains "socialist" in nature, even though the Chinese material economic system successfully made the transition from central planning to a market economy[45] and entered the "post-shortage period" by the end of the 1990s.[46]

When adopting some economic concepts, especially those from Kornai's economics of shortage, some caveats are necessary at the onset. First, unlike the material economy, which the Communists want to grow, the atheist ideology drives the Communist regimes to restrict religious supply, suppress religious demand, and eradicate religion when it is perceived as possible. Therefore, not all of the concepts and theorizing of Kornai's economics of shortage may be applied to the analysis of religious phenomena in Communist-ruled societies. Second, the religious-economic approach concerns only the process of exchange, not the nature of the religious "products" and "services," which the believers may hold holy, sacred, and separate from economic interest in the daily use of the term. I have no intention, implicit or explicit, of equating the religious economy with the material economy. Reductionism should be rejected and avoided, as religion is a complex social, psychological, and spiritual phenomenon.

Unlike most of the religious-economic studies in the existing literature, this book adopts a political-economic approach, which is especially important in the analysis of religious change in China. First, the Communists regard the ideology of Communism as a competitive alternative to religious beliefs, and vice versa. They have deliberately tried to replace conventional religion with the secular, atheist belief system of Communism. Actually, the religious subsystem in any society must compete with secularisms. Therefore, the religious economy should consider the factor of secularism, just as theologians would take the challenge of secularism seriously. Second, determined to stay in power, the Chinese Communist authorities are keen to suppress any social group that might become a rival or threat to its power, be it religious or not. The faith-based organizations are perceived as one of the most serious threats to the Communist Party. For instance, the Chinese Communist authorities regularly reiterate their fear of the Roman Catholic church as a serious threat, even though Catholics make up less than 1 percent of the Chinese population by anyone's estimate. The authorities have become paranoid regarding the roles that the Roman Catholic church played in the collapse of Communism in Poland. During my visits in China, I have had many conversations with government officials in various offices. They commonly shared the belief that the United States conspired with the Vatican to have a Polish-born pope, to instigate the Solidarity Movement, and eventually to overthrow the Communist rule. Moreover, they used this conspiracy theory to justify the harsh measures against the Catholic church and other religious sects in China. Meanwhile, the Chinese authorities also hold similar serious fears of sectarian groups such as the historical White Lotus Sect and dealt harshly with Falun Gong. Political scientist Christopher Marsh shows that many internal policies and official reports explicitly warn that China must "manage correctly religious affairs if it is to avoid" a Soviet-style collapse. He quotes Ye Xiaowen, the director of the State Administration of Religious Affairs for many years, as arguing that "religion became a weapon in the hands of the dissidents for inciting the masses and creating political disturbances."[47] Therefore, religion in China under

Communism is inevitably political, and thus it is necessary to adopt a political-economic approach to achieve a more accurate understanding of the complex situation.

Furthermore, to examine the full political economy of religion in China or elsewhere, it is necessary to include spiritual alternatives to institutionalized religion. Existing studies debating supply-side theories[48] have focused almost exclusively on one type of religiosity: religious participation in formal religious organizations in the form of membership and attendance. This is in part because of the fact that the religious supplies in North America and Europe are mostly from religious organizations and in part because of the concern by the involved researchers for quantification for mathematical modeling with neat measures. But reality is often not so neat. All societies have noninstitutionalized religious beliefs and practices, which include what have been variably called "popular religion," "folk religion," "primal religion," "implicit religion," "pseudo-religion," or "quasi-religion." Noninstitutionalized beliefs and practices are especially widespread in non-Western societies, in which religion is supplied not only by organized religions but also by individual shamans, witches, oracles, gurus, ritual specialists, and the like. Very often, such individual suppliers are not professional clergy or ecclesiastics but moonlighters. As will be shown in chapters 6 and 7 below, these noninstitutionalized spiritualities play important roles in China and probably also in other heavily regulated religious economies.

But what should be regarded as religion or religious and what should not? There is so much confusion on this matter among scholars and lay people. It is therefore unavoidable to seek clarification in the definition of religion before proceeding further with this social-scientific study of religion.

A DEFINITION OF RELIGION

FOR THE SOCIAL-SCIENTIFIC

STUDY OF RELIGION

DEFINITIONS MATTER. IN the West, many scholars define religion by expediency or pedagogical considerations,[1] avoiding it whenever possible, as Max Weber famously did while completing his series of studies of religions. In China, however, defining religion is not a simple matter in an ivory tower. For believers, a proper definition of religion has serious consequences for self-identification and sociopolitical classification that may affect the level of freedom or privileges in society. On the part of the government, a proper definition of religion may have direct relevance to maintaining social stability and the political order.

Indeed, the definition sometimes can be a matter of life and death. For instance, scholars outside China have commonly discussed Falun Gong as a religious group or a new religious movement,[2] in spite of the fact that followers of Falun Gong have insisted that it is not a religion. Being perceived as a nonreligious group, Falun Gong initially enjoyed much freedom in China in the 1990s, when government-recognized religions were strictly restricted by the authorities. In 1999, the Chinese government banned Falun Gong as a *xie jiao* (evil cult) and since then has adamantly rejected calling it a religion. To the Communist government, Falun Gong as an "evil cult" falls outside the constitutional protection of the freedom of religious belief; thus, the authorities claim it is justified to eradicate Falun Gong and similar groups in the entire society. Meanwhile, Falun Gong practitioners, although strongly rejecting the label of "evil cult," nonetheless maintain that it is not a religion, insisting that it is something much better than existing religions.

A question is thus inevitable for the social scientists of religion. Given that both the followers and the government refuse to call it a religion, shall we stop studying Falun Gong as a religious group? If we treat it as religious, as has been done multiple times for this and similar groups in Chinese and other societies, on what ground do we justify including it in the social category of religion? Admittedly, religion is a social construct subjected to negotiation among various groups of people, as scrupulously argued by British sociologist James A. Beckford. Beckford insists that "social scientists [should] distinguish between the 'first order' notions of religion that actors deploy in everyday life and the 'second order' constructs that serve analytical purposes. In both cases, ideas of what counts as religion are constructed, negotiated and contested."[3] This is true. But there is another, more powerful player at the negotiation table: the state, which defines through regulation what is and what is not religion. Canadian sociologist of religion Peter Beyer, comparing religions in the globalized world in modern times, distinguishes three types of conceptions of religion: scientific, theological, and "official."[4] Following this line of conceptualization, we may see that, broadly speaking, in the modern or modernizing world, there are three major social forces contending to define religion: scholars, believers, and the government.

The modern state is often pressed to make clear distinctions between religions and nonreligions for regulative or legal reasons. The nuanced, sophisticated, and scholastic reluctance to define religion is of no help in this regard. On the other hand, it is not rare to hear some followers of a particular group, such as Christianity, Buddhism, or Falun Gong, refuse the label of religion with their own theological rationales. Occasionally, some followers of a particular group, such as Scientology, claim to be religious, yet most people seem unwilling to concur. Any consensus definition of religion seems far beyond reach among the contenders of the followers, the state, and the academicians.

As social scientists, even though we admit that the "second order" constructs by scholars are for analytical purposes, nonetheless these constructs may have some important effect on the self-perception of believers and/or government regulations. Because of this real possibility, I believe that expediency is not the socially responsible strategy, nor do we have to resort to perpetual evasion. Social scientists may advance the knowledge and understanding of complex social phenomena by relying on scientific principles. If not for hustled convenience, scholars would normally take a detached position and attempt to define religion as objectively as possible, making it as universally applicable as possible. Certainly, as social persons living in a limited time and space, along with subjective constraints that no one can completely shake off, social scientists cannot totally avoid subjectivity. However, this should not become an excuse for not trying to be value-neutral as long as we try to engage in the scientific endeavor.

Social scientists do not have to give in to the postmodernist abandonment of science.

Therefore, for purposes of the social-scientific study of religion, in this chapter, I present a definition of religion. This is done so that the arguments in this book, or similar social-scientific studies, can retain an acceptable level of clarity, without which scholarly exchange will be impossible. Before presenting my own definition of religion, however, it is probably helpful to review the challenges and what has been done about defining religion for analytical purposes.

DEFINITIONS OF RELIGION IN SOCIAL SCIENCE

The definition of religion remains problematic in spite of conscientious efforts by many social scientists.[5] No one doubts that Max Weber is, among other things, a great sociologist of religion. However, Weber famously evaded the definition question: "To define 'religion,' to say what it *is*, is not possible at the start of a presentation such as this. Definition can be attempted, if at all, only at the conclusion of the study."[6] In the end, however, he states that the work has been done, and after all, there is no need to make a definition. However, his study of Confucianism and Daoism, translated into English and Chinese as *The Religion of China: Confucianism and Daoism,* raises more questions than answers. An important question is, in what sense can Confucianism be considered a religion while it is not recognized as a religion by the Chinese government or by most Chinese people?[7]

The recent introduction of social theories of religion by contemporary Western scholars is not of much help, either.

For example, renowned American sociologist of religion Robert Bellah speaks about civil religion without articulating the distinction between civil religion and conventional religions. This indeed adds confusion. It is even more confusing when many other academicians have published serious scholarship treating "sports as religion," "politics as religion," or "capitalism as religion,"[8] although normally these are not considered religion at all.

Attempting clarification and contextualization, many scholars have made meticulous examinations of the etymology of religion, including the importation of the term *zongjiao* into the Chinese language around the turn of the twentieth century.[9] However, religion as a system of beliefs, moral teachings, and practices in an observable social institution is a modern or recent understanding not only to the Chinese and Japanese but also to Westerners. According to Wilfred Cantwell Smith, this meaning of the word became solidified in the seventeenth to nineteenth centuries in the West when the expanding West encountered systems in other societies that are comparable to Christianity.[10] Certainly, a historicized and contextualized understanding of the meaning of the term *religion* can be informative and keep things in perspective, but that understanding should not become a pretext to cripple the scientific effort to construct a definition of religion that may be universally applicable for analytical purposes.

It is important to emphasize that in social science, no truth claim can be made in a definition. Recognizing the normative implications of a scholarly definition in its interaction with the state and followers, a social-science definition tries to focus on the descriptive nature of the definition and ought to be as value-free as possible. Definitions and propositions are no more than theoretical tools for handling the empirical phenomena. Tools in themselves cannot be said to be right or wrong. But some tools are more useful than others for particular tasks. When people apply improper or wrong tools, they may fail to handle the things on which they are working, or they may labor hard to little avail. The carpenter's tools are not very useful for the blacksmith, and the horticulturalist's tools cannot be effective for stonemasons. Tools should be evaluated by their usefulness for a given task.[11] Further, a useful set of tools may nonetheless need improvements to some of the specific implements. As I will argue below, Durkheim's definition of religion is a useful conceptual tool, but it requires some improvements for the purpose of research on religion in the modern world.

Among the empirical studies of religion by social scientists, American psychologist William James was interested in personal religion, that is, feelings, acts, and experiences of individuals in their solitude in relation to whatever they may consider the divine.[12] Religious experiences are certainly individually experienced, and some of the most profound experiences are so personal and private that no words can convey their fullness. Nevertheless, religious experiences are socially conditioned.

Seeing religion as fundamentally a social phenomenon, sociologists often distinguish two types of definitions of religion: substantive and functional.[13] A substantive definition points to the belief in the supernatural or the transcendent; a functional definition describes what religion does. Historically, E. B. Tylor simply defined religion as "the belief in Spiritual Beings,"[14] which is regarded as the first substantive type, while Emile Durkheim's definition is often considered functionalist: "A religion is a unified system of beliefs and practices relative to sacred things, that is to say, things set apart and surrounded by prohibitions—beliefs and practices which unite its adherents in a single moral community called a Church."[15]

In his attempt to stay away from the substantive definition that seems biased in favor of theistic religion, Durkheim adopts the more inclusive term *sacred* as an essential element of religion by citing atheistic Buddhism. Durkheim claims, "In the first place, there are great religions in which the idea of gods and spirits is absent, or plays only a secondary and unobtrusive role. This is the case with Buddhism."[16] Therefore, "the sacred things" are merely things that are set apart and surrounded by prohibitions, which may include all kinds of ordinary things, such as certain birds or animals in totemism.

But Durkheim goes overboard with the aloofness in his definition, because atheistic Buddhism could be claimed by no more than an exceptionally few philosophical minds. The vast majority of Buddhists do, in fact, believe in spiritual beings, including the Buddha as an extraordinary and super-human being.[17] The functionalist embellishment of the "sacred," indeed its further diluting, is exacerbated in the often quoted definition of religion by anthropologist Clifford Geertz: "a system of symbols which acts to establish powerful, pervasive, and long-lasting moods and motivations in men by formulating conceptions of a general order of existence and clothing these conceptions with such an aura of factuality that the moods and motivations seem uniquely realistic."[18] In many respects, this definition is so inclusive that nationalism, economics, music, sports, and so on, could easily fit into the same: "Geertz points out that his definition of religion would include, for example, golf—not if a person merely played it with a passion, but rather if golf were seen as symbolic of some transcendent order."[19] Unfortunately, such an inclusive definition renders "religion" devoid of precision. When so many vastly different things are studied all under the name of "religion," the term has become like a dumping container. Anything may be thrown into it, but it becomes anything but a meaningful analytical tool for the scientific endeavor.

While the "sacred" is too generic, Durkheim's use of "church" in his definition is particularistic in appearance, as it is usually associated with Christianity, yet he defines "church" too broadly: "A society whose members are united because they share a common conception of the sacred world and its relation to the profane world, and who translate this common conception into identical practices, is what we call a church."[20] He stretches such a society to include a nation, an ethnicity, a family, and a guild, as well as a fraction of a population. This expansive definition may account for certain social facts in historical times. But its direct application to a modern society causes confusion, as in the popular conceptualization of civil religion in America by Robert Bellah and the similarly popular conceptualization of "diffused religion" in Chinese society by C. K. Yang. Durkheim is right to designate the collective nature of religion: a religion is defined in terms of a moral association of people who share beliefs and practices and have a sense of belonging to this group. However, Durkheim's primary image of one society with one religion was archaic, and his focus on primitive societies reinforced that image. But the lack of institutional differentiation is characteristic of the primitive society, not of the modern society, as analyzed by Durkheim himself.

In order to see clearly the elementary forms of religion that are essential, Durkheim uses the empirical materials of the Australian aboriginals. Durkheim states in the onset, "In this book we propose to study the most primitive and simplest religion currently known . . . because it seems most likely to yield an understanding of the religious nature of man, by showing us an essential and permanent aspect of humanity."[21] Examining a tribal society's "religion" was for the purpose of understanding religion in general. "It is indeed useful to know what a particular religion is about, yet it is far more important to discover what religion is in general. . . . At the basis of all systems of belief and all cults there must be a certain number of fundamental representations and ritual practices that, despite the diversity of forms they assume in the various religions, have the same objective meanings and fulfill the same functions. It is these permanent elements that constitute something eternal and human in religion; they provide the objective content of the idea that is expressed when we speak of *religion* in general."[22]

Durkheim believed that he could discover the permanent elements of religion in general through the examination of tribal societies. However, it is important to recognize that the elementary or primitive form of religion has undergone broad transformations in later development, especially during the modernization process. Religion has increasingly become an institution with differentiated, separate, and observable organizations. While totemism helps Durkheim to articulate his theory of religion in general, totemism is not the dominant form of religion within modern societies. In the West, the Reformation broke down the myth of the holistic religious society. In China, multiple religions have coexisted for thousands of years.

It is important to stress the modern developments of religion. First, the institutional differentiation in the process of modernization has increasingly made religion conceivably a separate social institution from other institutions of politics, economy, the family, education, and so on. Second, the coexistence of plural religions in a society is characteristic of modern times. Religion has become a noun that has to be understood as a plural one in almost all societies that have gone beyond the primitive stage. The time of the whole society adhering to a single religion is long gone, if it ever existed, such as in some primitive tribes or societies. The seeming religiously homogeneous or monopolistic societies today are those that refuse to admit the existence of alternative religions or refuse to grant the freedom for individuals to go their own ways in their spiritual pursuits. In modern times, Durkheim admits, the pluralization of religion in European societies has redefined a church as a fraction of a population, which he speaks of as the "Christian societies since the advent of Protestantism."[23] Nowadays these are commonly referred to as "denominations" and "sects." The organizational form of religion has moved away from the undifferentiated form in primitive societies.

Following Durkheim's study of the primitive societies, C. K. Yang's *Religion in Chinese Society* focuses on what he defines as "diffused religion" in contrast to institutional religions. The significant contribution of this seminal work is its empirical evidence that effectively debunked the widespread belief or myth of the irreligious nature of the Chinese culture, a misperception created by the elitist intellectuals in modern times in response to the Western Enlightenment modernity. However, treating the religious elements in traditional social life as *a* religion comparable to institutional religions has generated more confusion than clarification for scholarly research since Yang's publication. It has become a perennial problem about the nature of folk practices that are of a religious nature. Is there a "Chinese religion" to the Chinese, as there is Hinduism to the Indians? At least part of the problem results from Yang's presentation. He seems to treat the Chinese religious life as very much static and fossilized and appearing to be fundamentally different from religious life in Western societies. This dominant interpretation of Yang is ironic, because the empirical materials are drawn from the late Qing and Republic periods when China was undergoing dramatic and profound social changes. One of the significant social changes was that sectarian movements flourished in postdynastic modern China.[24] These sectarian movements have differentiated social organizations in their religious beliefs and practices, no longer diffused into other social institutions.

Following C. K. Yang's distinction of institutional and diffused religions without a historical perspective, some scholars have fallen into the trap of exceptionalism in timeless China, insisting on the uniqueness of Chinese religion, as discussed above in chapter 1. As social scientists, we should not lose sight of and ignore social and religious change. Even if the so-called diffused religion was once the dominant form of religion in historical China, that does not mean that it will remain so in modern China. One of the major tasks of social scientists is to seek to discover the social reasons that the "diffused religion" was prevalent in premodern China, why sectarian movements arose in the early Republic of China, and how and why religion has changed in China today. Such a task requires a more refined definition of religion.

A DEFINITION OF RELIGION WITH CLASSIFICATION

For the purpose of the social-scientific study of religion in contemporary society, the definition of religion must be a simple abstraction that is broad enough to include all religions but sufficiently specific to distinguish religion from other similar concepts. Based on the simple definition by Durkheim but integrating the substantive character articulated by Tylor and many other scholars, I propose this definition of religion: *A religion is a unified system of beliefs and practices about life and the world relative to the supernatural that unite the believers or followers into a social organization of moral community.*

This definition includes four essential elements of a religion: (1) a belief in the supernatural, (2) a set of beliefs regarding life and the world, (3) a set of ritual practices manifesting the beliefs, and (4) a distinct social organization of moral community of believers and practitioners.

From this definition, we will develop a classification of religious phenomena and closely related social phenomena that compete with religion (see table 2.1).

The first type in the classification scheme may be called *full religion*. Scholars have tried other names. In his classic work *The Scientific Study of Religion*, J. Milton Yinger mentions the "complete" religion.[25] In her popular textbook *Religion in America*, Julia Corbett Hemeyer distinguishes the "developed" and underdeveloped religions: "A *Developed Religion* is an integrated system of beliefs, lifestyle, ritual activities, and social institutions by which individuals give meaning to (or find meaning in) their lives by orienting themselves to what they take to be holy, sacred, or of the

Table 2.1

A DEFINITION OF RELIGION WITH CLASSIFICATION

	Supernatural	Beliefs	Practices	Organization	Examples
Full religion	Yes	Yes	Yes	Yes	Christianity, Buddhism, Islam
Semireligion	Yes	Underdeveloped	Yes	Underdeveloped	Folk or popular religion, magic, spiritualities
Quasi-religion	Yes	Yes	Yes	Diffused	Civil religion, ancestor worship, guild cults
Pseudo-religion	No	Yes	Yes	Yes	Atheism, Communism, fetishism

highest value."[26] Here I call it full religion if it clearly has all four of the essential elements.

If a group has all four elements but some of them are underdeveloped, we may call it a *semireligion,* which may have the potential to develop into a full religion. When one of the four essential elements is missing, if the label of religion is to be used at all, such a group is more properly called a *quasi-religion* or a *pseudo-religion.* Unlike semireligions, at least in modern times, quasi- and pseudo-religions cannot develop into full religions. This will become clear in further explanation below, after discussing religion and magic, another perennial difficulty with which scholars of religions have to deal.

Among the four elements, the supernatural can be a being or beings, a mystical force or forces. Using "supernatural" instead of "spiritual beings" intentionally blurs the distinction between religion and magic in this dimension. This is in line with classic sociologists of religion. For Weber, charisma is a common characteristic of religion and magic.[27] For Durkheim,

> Magic also consists of beliefs and rites. Like religion, it has myths and its dogmas, but they are more rudimentary, probably because in pursuing technical and utilitarian aims, magic does not waste time in pure speculation. Magic also has its ceremonies, sacrifices, purification rituals, prayers, chants, and dances. The beings invoked by the magician, the forces he puts into play, are not only similar in nature to the forces and beings addressed by religion but often identical... the souls of the dead, their bones and their hair, are among the magician's most useful tools. Demons are also commonly used in the performance of magic. Now, demons, too, are beings surrounded by prohibitions; they too are

separated, living in a world apart, and it is often difficult to distinguish them from gods proper....The magician even invokes regular and official divinities...the Virgin, Christ, and the saints have been used in the same way by Christian magicians."[28]

If so much is the same between magic and religion in terms of appealing to spiritual beings or supernatural forces, what makes magic and religion distinct? What is the demarcation line between magic and religion? Following Durkheim, the key distinction lies in the social organization: "Magic does not bind its followers to one another and unite them in a single group living the same life. *A church of magic does not exist.* Between the magician and his followers, and between these individuals themselves, there are no lasting bonds that make them members of a moral body like the one formed by worshippers of the same god. The magician has a clientele, not a church, and his clients may well be entirely unrelated and even unaware of each other; even their relations with him are generally accidental and transitory, like those of a patient with his doctor."[29] In other words, the key difference is that magic lacks the moral association of believers or practitioners. Of course, it is difficult to devise a classification scheme that can put everything in a proper, clean, and neat place. There are always cases that seem to be in-betweens of different categories. In a historical perspective, some people of a conglomeration of magic, especially those in primitive societies, may develop into a moral community, thus turning magic into religion. In reality, we may find that certain groups are in the process of evolving toward becoming a full-fledged religion.

Moreover, in the real life of believers and practitioners, whether some rite is religious or magical often depends on how the subjects perceive it at the moment. For example, praying for healing can be religious, pleading and seeking discernment without commanding, and it can be magical, trying to perform the rites methodically in order to manipulate the spiritual force or beings. The Bible may be read for a developed understanding or discerning of the Holy Spirit, and it may also be placed on the bed to fend off evil spirits, and the same person may do both. Historically, magic is often part and parcel of the institutional religion. Ronald Johnstone writes: "Thus, magic is probably best seen neither as a competitor with religion nor as an alternative to it, but as a specialized subunit of religion. In fact, rarely is religion without at least some magical elements, just as magic is seldom practiced entirely apart from a larger religious system that legitimates it."[30] In contemporary society, in the eyes of outsiders, the Catholic, charismatic, or Pentecostal Christians continue to have many magical elements integrated into their routine religious activities. Therefore, strictly distinguishing magic and religion is not necessary for the purpose of the social-scientific study of religion. Of course, the moral effects of religion or the lack of them in magic, as discussed by Durkheim, Weber, and many other classic thinkers, may still hold and should be examined more closely, but that is not the focus of this book.

This definition with classification combines substantive and functional definitions of religion and encompasses conventional religions and their competitors in modern society. The competitors, besides conventional religions and semireligions, also include pseudo-religions that are regarded as substitutes for conventional religions and quasi-religious beliefs and practices that are inseparable from other social institutions.

The semireligions are underdeveloped religions that include a wide range of things, from animism to shamanism, from totemism to tutelage cults. Some of these are more developed than others. The rationalization tendency leads some of these into new religions, such as new paganism and Falun Gong, or into certain kinds of integration with a conventional religion. Both Catholicism and charismatic Protestantism have successfully absorbed various "primal" religious symbols, practices, and beliefs. Some groups may make intentional efforts to develop their belief system and organization. But most semireligious phenomena remain underdeveloped. Such beliefs and practices are doubtless religious. They even have certain kinds of organization, although they are often temporary arrangements and undifferentiated from other social institutions. Besides, both the practitioners and the researchers tend to have difficulties in coming up with certain cohesive names, other than naming them after locations. In many parts of China, there are "communal religions" that look alike across regions, but each local community maintains a different set of gods, spirits, good books, and rituals.[31] Such folk-religious practices are classified as semireligions in this scheme.

Quasi-religions are also diffused religions, but they are intrinsically embedded in other institutions without a stand-alone organization. For example, civil religion is inseparable from the state, ancestor worship from the family, and vocation cults from the trade guilds. The diffused religion, as rightly argued by C. K. Yang, often borrows religious symbols, rites, and ideas from institutional religions, and through diffused religion some people may also be drawn into an institutional religion. Therefore, quasi-religion may either compete with or complement the institutional religion or do both simultaneously. The primary function of diffused religion is to reinforce the secular institution to which it is attached.[32] On the other hand, because it is so much embedded or even parasitic, when the old state, the family, or the guild collapses, the corresponding quasi-religion will also collapse, leaving residual fragments in folklores.

The key element missing in a pseudo-religion is belief in the supernatural. It may believe in something sacred, or something is artificially made sacred, that is, set apart and surrounded by prohibitions, such as the state or some "ism," but that sacred something is not a supernatural being or a supernatural force. Pseudo-religions may generate real sentiments and devolution just as conventional religions do. In modern times, various secularisms, including atheism, scientism, and Communism, have been perceived by some people as substitutes for religion. Some social and political forces have tried to force such religious substitutes on people in their wars against all religion. We emphasize here the descriptive nature of the social-scientific definition without claiming that religion itself is innately better than pseudo-religious systems. We define it in this way because our research focus here is on religion. For a study that focuses on ideology, religion might be defined as a pseudo-ideology or a false consciousness in the superstructure of ideology in Marxist terms. Indeed, religion has been often treated as an epiphenomenon without its own substance. Recognizing the normative implication of the prefix *pseudo-*, we can nonetheless understand it objectively, as *pseudo-* can be perceived as neither good nor bad, when it is associated with culturally neutral words such as *pseudocoel* or *pseudonym*.

This definition with classification is a useful tool in the political economy of religion that deals with conventional religions and their active competitors in the same society. In a study focusing on the survival and revival of religions in Communist-ruled China, the distinction between religion and pseudo-religion is especially important. In China, as in other Communist-ruled societies, the pseudo-religion of Communism was forced on the people as a substitute for religion, but many people resorted to some semireligion that would provide the supernatural element. Because of the lack of formal organizations or the elusive nature of the organizational element in popular religion or folk religion, it is more difficult for authorities to suppress such practices and beliefs.

Finally, this definition of religion with classification also indicates that religious freedom is not just the freedom to hold religious beliefs but also the freedom to engage in religious practices and to join in religious organizations. In China, while the Communist officials have circumspectly maintained that the Constitution of the People's Republic of China protects the freedom of religious beliefs, they have often intentionally left out the other two elements of religion to justify the restrictive regulations. In the next two chapters, we will examine the evolution of the Chinese Communist understanding of religion and its corresponding religious regulations.

CHINESE MARXIST ATHEISM AND

ITS POLICY IMPLICATIONS

IN CHINA, THE Communist authorities understand religion on the basis of Marxist atheism: the essence of religion is the spiritual opium of the people, and its destiny is to wither away. Since the late 1970s, however, Chinese religious researchers have become formidable forces of contention over the definition and essence of religion. In response, Marxist atheism has evolved into multiple forms, each of which has different implications for religious policy.

VARIOUS FORMS OF ATHEISM

In the ideological lexicon of the Chinese Communist Party (CCP), Marxist-Leninist atheism is a fundamental doctrine. Since 1921, when the CCP was established, Chinese Communist atheism has taken two major forms: enlightenment atheism and militant atheism. A third form of atheism has emerged recently, self-designated as mild atheism. All of these forms of atheism have their specific adherents and advocates. Lü Daji, a senior research fellow at the Institute of World Religions at the Chinese Academy of Social Sciences, is an exemplar of people who have shifted away from militant atheism toward enlightenment atheism; Gong Xuezeng, a professor at the Central School of the Chinese Communist Party, has been an outspoken militant atheist; and Mou Zhongjian, a professor at the Central University for Nationalities (*Minzu Daxue*), has recently articulated *wenhe wushenlun* (mild atheism). While all of these theoreticians claim to be Marxist and to maintain Marxist orthodoxy, in practice, these different forms of atheism would lead to very different policies toward religion. Militant atheism leads to antireligious measures, enlightenment atheism serves as the theoretical basis for a limited tolerance of religion while insisting on atheist propaganda, and mild atheism justifies an even greater tolerance of religion.

Enlightenment atheism regards religion as an illusory or false consciousness, being both nonscientific and backward; thus, atheist propaganda is necessary to expunge the misleading religious ideas. In comparison, militant atheism treats religion as the dangerous opium and narcotic of the people, a wrong political ideology serving the interests of the exploiting classes and the antirevolutionary elements; thus, political forces are necessary to control and eliminate religion. In other words, if enlightenment atheism hopes for a decline in religious doctrine through scientific development, mass education, and propaganda, militant atheism sees a need to take greater social and political measures to control and eradicate religion. While the former may imply some pity for and sympathy to the believers and consent to a certain degree of tolerance of existing religions, the latter regards religious believers, leaders, and organizations as counterrevolutionary forces that should be restricted, reduced, and eliminated. Both kinds of atheism can be found in the sanctified writings of Marx, Engels, Lenin, Stalin, and Mao. Militant atheism shows up more blatantly in the writings of Lenin and other Russian Bolsheviks, whereas enlightenment atheism has deep roots in the European Enlightenment movement.

The Enlightenment and Bolshevism are entwined heritages of the CCP. Founded in 1921, the CCP emerged after the May Fourth movement in 1919 or the broader New Culture movement that arose around the same time. The main thrusts of the May Fourth or New Culture movement include calling for adopting democracy and science in Chinese society and iconoclastic antitraditionalism, as epitomized in the slogan "Down with the Confucian shops." Influenced by the Enlightenment and modern Western philosophies, many leading intellectuals engaged in fierce attacks on religion and the traditional culture, and some leading thinkers recommended replacing religion with science, ethics, or aesthetic education. Meanwhile, "the salvoes of the Russian October Revolution brought us Marxism-Leninism," as is commonly said in China. Some of the influential leaders of the New Culture movement adopted Marxism-Leninism. Among them, Chen Duxiu and Li Dazhao became founders of the CCP and kindled young people into aggressive attacks on religion.

After the establishment of the People's Republic of China (PRC) in 1949, the new Communist regime drew heavily on Soviet sources regarding religion.[1] On October 18, 1950, the *Renmin Ribao (People's Daily)* published an extensive review of two recent books. One, *Socialism and Religion*, includes Lenin's writings and some articles from the *Encyclopedia of the Soviet Union*. The other, *Selected Writings on the Problem of Religion*, includes excerpts from Engels, Stalin, William Z. Foster (the leader of the U.S. Communist Party), and some

Chinese Marxist-Leninist theoreticians. These textual sources amplified militant atheism and called for the eradication of religion by resolute measures.

In 1956, a long article, "Marxism-Leninism on the Religious Problem," by Tang Yao was published in the *Journal of Philosophical Research*. This is probably the first systematic articulation of the Marxist-Leninist view of religion by a Chinese theoretician. Tang states that the essence of religious ideas is the distorted, illusionary reflection of social reality. Therefore, religion is the opium of the people. Like opium, religion may provide a temporary comfort and permit a dismissal of suffering, but it will also seduce people into addiction, leading them to physical and psychological debilitation and thus rendering them submissive to the exploiters. Religion is always employed as a tool of exploitation of the people in the hands of the ruling class. Tang emphasizes the fundamental antagonism between religion and Communism. Accordingly, the CCP must carry out uncompromising struggles against religious superstitions.[2] In 1963, "Some Issues of the Marxist-Leninist View of Religion" by You Xiang and Liu Junwang was published in the magazine *New Construction*. These writers assert that the core of the Marxist-Leninist view of religion is to expose the reactionary essence of religion as the opium of the people. Religion will always act as poisonous opium and cannot but serve to obstruct the socialist endeavor. In a follow-up article published in 1964 in *Red Flag*, the official organ of the CCP, they called for a weakening of religious influences among the people and acceleration of the termination of religion. They stressed that the policy of freedom of religion was not designed to allow religion to restrain the masses. Such militant atheism preceded the eradication policy during the Cultural Revolution beginning in 1966.

THE NEW "OPIUM WAR" AMONG MARXIST THEORETICIANS

In the first three decades of the PRC, academic research on religion was no more than a means for atheist propaganda. A Chinese scholar, Dai Kangsheng, who lived through that period, states: "Scholarly research on religion was considered an important means for atheist education to the masses of the people, thus it stressed the differences and conflicts between theism and atheism, and between idealism and materialism."[3] He further says:

> During the Cultural Revolution [1966–1976], under the slogans of class struggles and the guiding principle of completely breaking up conventional ideas, religion was listed as part of the four olds [old ideas, old culture, old customs, and old habits] and of feudalism, capitalism and revisionism that should be eradicated. Religious beliefs of the great masses were said to be reflections of class struggles in the sphere of ideology and signs of political backwardness and reaction; religious believers were cracked down as ox-monsters and snake-demons, resulting in many framed and fabricated cases. Religion was a realm of heavy catastrophes. The Religious Affairs Bureau was dissolved; the cadres of religious affairs were censured for their crime of following the wrong political line. All religious venues were closed down. Many religious artifacts were destroyed. Religious research completely halted. The criticism of theism quickly became in practice the theoretical declaration for struggling and eliminating religion in society.[4]

This assessment is indisputable and shared by the researchers who lived through the period.

Following the death of Mao Zedong in 1976, Deng Xiaoping emerged as the paramount leader of the CCP and declared the end of the Cultural Revolution. At the end of 1978, the CCP launched economic reforms and open-door policies. As political pragmatism prevailed over ideological dogmatism, enlightenment atheism also prevailed over militant atheism.

The embodiment of enlightenment atheism is found in the CCP circular "The Basic Viewpoint and Policy on the Religious Affairs during the Socialist Period of Our Country."[5] Commonly known as Document No. 19 of 1982, this CCP circular has served as the foundation of religious policy from that time forth. It states that religion in socialist China has five characteristics: it (1) will exist for a long time, (2) has masses of believers, (3) is complex, (4) entwines with ethnicity, and (5) affects international relations. As a result of such characteristics, religious affairs must therefore be handled with care; religious believers should be rallied for the central task of economic construction, and religious freedom should be guaranteed as long as the believers love the country, support CCP's rule, and observe socialist laws. Document No. 19 acknowledges the mistakes of militant atheism. But it also clearly reaffirms the atheist doctrine: religion will eventually wither away, and atheist propaganda must be carried out unremittingly, albeit not inside religious venues. The authors of this document do admit the reality of religious persistence but note that the reduced proportion of religious believers in the whole population can be viewed as a partial victory of atheist propaganda. However, the persistence of religion—despite eradication measures and powerful propagandas—was both puzzling and troubling to the Marxist theoreticians. In addition to its roots in social classes, as asserted by the-then-understood Marxism-Leninism, Document No. 19 concedes, without elaboration, that religion may have psychological and social roots. The Chinese Communist document, while providing the basis for the limited tolerance policy, set off debates among Marxist theoreticians on the nature and roots of religion.

The debates started initially over the ideas behind the "opium" thesis. Is Marx's statement that "religion is the opium of the people" the core, cornerstone, and foundation of Marxist atheism? Under the cloud of thought liberation, some theoreticians spoke out their doubts. Many Marxist-Leninist theoreticians and academic scholars were drawn into the debates through numerous publications.[6] There were roughly two camps: the leftist camp was based primarily in Beijing at the Institute of World Religions (IWR) at the Chinese Academy of Social Sciences, and the liberal camp was loosely clustered in Shanghai and Nanjing, although there were also liberals in the north and leftists in the south. The left-leaning theoreticians insisted that the opium thesis was the cornerstone of the Marxist view of religion, whereas the liberal-leaning theoreticians and scholars offered counterarguments within the parameters of upholding orthodox Marxism, making painstaking efforts with delicate rhetoric. They argued effectively, in summary, that the opium statement is only an analogy, and an analogy is not a definition; the opium analogy by Marx should not be understood in completely negative terms, because opium was used as a pain reliever in Marx's time; this analogical statement does not represent the complete view of Marxism on religion, and Marx, as well as Engels, made other important statements on religion; and this is not a uniquely Marxist view, because other people before Marx had already compared religion to opium.

Eventually, the liberal-leaning understanding reigned among most religious researchers. After several years of debates, many leftist theoreticians softened their positions. Some of them even abandoned their original positions. In this regard, the position shifts of Lü Daji are exemplary. Lü has been a research fellow of the IWR since it became functional in the late 1970s. Initially, he was one of the major outspoken theoreticians of the northern leftist camp, who followed Lenin's emphasis that the opium statement was the cornerstone of the Marxist view of religion. By the end of the 1980s, however, Lü publicly moved away from that position. Still insisting on following orthodox Marxism, Lü took a statement from Engels as the key to defining religion. Engels, the cofounder of Marxism, says in *Anti-Dühring*, "All religion, however, is nothing but the illusory reflection in men's minds of those external forces which control their daily life, a reflection in which the terrestrial forces assume the form of supernatural forces."

Following this line of thought but expanding on it to include additional elements from Durkheim and other Western scholars, Lü offered this definition of religion in 1989: "Religion is a kind of social consciousness, an illusory reflection in people's minds of the external forces which control their daily life, a reflection in which the terrestrial forces assume the form of superhuman and supernatural forces, and the consequent believing and worshipping behaviors toward such forces; it is the normalized social-cultural system that synthesizes their consciousness and behaviors."[7] This is clearly an atheist definition of religion, because it presumes that all gods are illusory beings. But it has also clearly moved away from Leninist militant atheism. Lü's book *A General Theory of Religious Studies*, published in 1989, was praised by many scholars of religious research in China.

About a decade later, Lü further discredited Engels's statement. First, Lü said that the statement was a value judgment, biased by a strong atheist position, thus unacceptable as a scientific definition. The scientific definition should be value-neutral or value-free and should not negate at the onset the existence of god or gods. Second, this statement was only about the notion of god, not about the whole of religion, which should include the social organization, as well as the religious ideas. Therefore, the definition of religion was refor-mulated: "Religion is a kind of social consciousness regarding superhuman and supernatural forces, and its consequent believing and worshipping behaviors toward such forces; it is the normalized and institutionalized social-cultural system that synthesizes this consciousness and the behaviors."[8]

By then, Lü did not insist that this was a Marxist defini-tion. Instead, he stated that it was a scientific definition with reference to various theories of religion, including both Marxist and non-Marxist ones. More important, it seemed not to matter anymore whether the definition was Marxist or not. As Lü contended, "We should not indiscreetly negate a view or blindly accept a stand." He even expressed an appre-ciation for the belief in gods because of its liberating effects on primitive people. Obviously, this new definition of reli-gion and the corresponding new attitudes that have arisen from it have come a long way. What is interesting in Lü's per-spective is that, instead of being reprimanded by the author-ities for his open departure from Marxist orthodoxy, Lü's definition has been widely praised by scholars of religious research for its scientific nature and liberating effect from ideological dogmatism.

Chinese scholars have referred to the debates on the def-inition and essence of religion as the new "opium war" because of the involvement of numerous people and its social and political implications. However, the real contribution of this "opium war" was probably that it legitimized religious research as an academic discipline and stimulated research interest in religion among young scholars. The Institute of World Religions at the Chinese Academy of Social Sciences expanded, and some provincial academies of social sciences established religious research institutes, including Shanghai in 1980, Yunnan in 1984, and Tibet in 1985. Several specialty journals for religious research were launched, including the *Journal for the Study of World Religions* (Beijing, 1979), *Religion* (Nanjing, 1979), *Sources of World Religions* (Beijing, 1980), *Scholarly Research on Religion* (Chengdu, 1982), *Contemporary Religious Research* (Shanghai, 1989), and several others for internal circulation. Meanwhile, several major universities, including Fudan University, Nanjing University, Wuhan University, Renmin University of China, and Peking University, have formed divisions for teaching and studying religion based in philosophy departments. I myself joined the faculty of philosophy at Renmin University of China when the division was put together in 1987. Some books have also been published to introduce various religions and histories of Chinese Buddhism, Daoism, Islam, and Christian missions. Throughout the 1980s, the overall tone of the publications gradually changed from a completely negative criticism of religion to an increasingly balanced evaluation.

"RELIGION IS CULTURE!"

Following the end of the Cultural Revolution, the Thought Liberation campaigns rehabilitated *culture* as an esteemed term. An effervescence of cultural discussions spread widely in academia throughout the 1980s. Amid the culture craze, some scholars of religious research championed the study of religion as an essential part of culture.[9] In the 1990s, the cultural approach to religion made vivacious waves. Several new journals were launched, including *Buddhist Culture* (Beijing, 1989) and the *Review of Christian Culture* (Guiyang, 1990). The well-established journal *Sources of World Religions* was renamed *World Religious Culture* in 1995. Several "journals in book form" (*yi shu dai kan*) appeared, including *Religion and Culture* (Hangzhou, 1994) and the *Collections of Studies of Christian Culture* (Beijing, 1999). Meanwhile, several publishers brought forth series of books: *Religious Culture Popular Readings* by Qilu Press,[10] *Religious Culture* by China Construction Press,[11] and the *Religion and the World* translation series by Sichuan People's Press, which includes a variety of scholarly books in humanities and the social sciences. A newly established publisher was even named the Religious Culture Press.[12] Regarding the significance of the cultural turn in religious research, Lü Daji says, "In reviewing the path of scholarship on religious research since 1949 we may say this: there has been no other theory or concept but religion is reactionary politics that is more constraining to scholars of religious research; and there has been no other theory or concept but religion is culture that is more liberating to scholars of religious research."[13] This is a precise observation indeed.

The importance of the cultural approach to religious research is twofold. First, when religion is studied as a cultural phenomenon, its ideological incorrectness becomes unimportant and its scientific incorrectness obscured, eliminating two key criticisms of religion by both militant and enlightenment atheism. Culture has its own significance and its own life. Religion as part of culture has its own reasons for existence and its own course of change. Studying religion as culture, therefore, is necessary and respectable. Second, the cultural approach makes religious research more wide-reaching and consequently academically rewarding. Scholars of both religious research and other disciplines can now write and publish works about religion and its related aspects of culture and society, such as the arts, philosophy, literature, education, politics, archeology, and science. The topics are limitless, and the new book series and new journals provide outlets for such scholarly studies. The effervescence of cultural discourses of religion, in effect, pushes the atheist advocates to the margins of academia. Militant atheism has receded to the chambers of the CCP schools. In the 1990s, several major universities established departments of religious studies, including Peking University, Renmin University of China, Fudan University, and Wuhan University.

During this time, some scholars have become either openly sympathetic to religion in general or to a particular religion. The phenomenon of cultural Christians (*Wenhua Jidutu*) is the most interesting development in this regard. In the past, Chinese intellectuals in general were most critical of Christianity, working with the perception of Christianity as a foreign religion and a means of Western colonialism and imperialism.[14] In the 1990s, however, quite a number of Chinese scholars began to publish works regarding Christianity with greater sympathy and empathy.[15] Some of these scholars have even openly or semiopenly taken up the Christian faith themselves. These scholars are commonly based in universities and research academies in the disciplines of philosophy, history, and literature. They have translated Western books of Christian theology, philosophy, and history into the Chinese language; published books and articles about Christianity; and lectured on university campuses to introduce Christianity into academia. It is the cultural approach that has legitimized such activities within the varied academic settings, for such scholars often can claim to be studying and introducing Western culture itself and not religion per se. These cultural Christians have stirred up a Christianity fashion or fad among college-educated urbanites while underground house churches spread with zeal in the rural areas. Many college students and intellectuals have been drawn to Christianity initially through reading the publications of the cultural Christian intellectuals, rather than through contact with churches or Christian believers. Because of their prolific publications and enthusiastic promotion of Christianity, the cultural Christians have been dubbed China's Apollos by outside observers.[16] According to the Book of Acts (18: 24–28) in the New Testament, Apollos was a Jewish teacher and follower of John the Baptist but became an enthusiastic and effective preacher of the Christian gospel even before his Christian baptism.

Besides the so-called cultural Christians, a greater number of scholars are openly sympathetic to or believing in Buddhism. Therefore, lately, some people have begun talking about a comparable phenomenon of cultural Buddhists within academia. Actually, there have also been academic scholars who are committed Muslims and who are passionate about Daoism.

THE PERSISTENCE OF MILITANT ATHEISM AND RESISTANCE OF ACADEMICIANS

While academicians have become increasingly open to various theories of religion, the CCP has not wavered from the atheist stand. In the reform era, when speaking to the outside world, Chinese officials have commonly made statements in accordance with the international norm of affirming religious freedom. Internally, however, CCP theoreticians have never shied away from explicit expressions of atheism but rather have reinforced atheism as a Marxist orthodoxy throughout CCP schools, internal circulars, and periodic propaganda campaigns. Ye Xiaowen, the director of the State Administration of Religious Affairs between 1995 and 2009, acted as the spokesperson to the outside world about the status of religious freedom in China. However, when he spoke at the CCP Central Party School in 1997, he made his atheist position clear: "We always hope to gradually weaken the influence of religion."[17] Such a statement is very revealing of the official stand of the CCP regarding religion.

Atheism continues to be reaffirmed as the Marxist orthodoxy. To take one recent example, Gong Xuezeng is arguably the most authoritative CCP theoretician on religion in China today. He has held the professorship of religious studies at the Central School of the CCP, which provides short-term training for both upper- and upper-middle-ranked CCP officials. In his 2003 book, *Socialism and Religion,*[18] he appears to have carefully reviewed a number of writings from Marx and Engels relevant to religion and summarizes the key points of the Marxist view of religion as follows:

1. Religion is a kind of social consciousness belonging to the superstructure that is determined by the economic base.
2. The essence of religion is the illusionary and upside-down reflection of the external forces dominating people's daily life.

3. The roots of religion must be searched for in the objective reality of life, especially in the reality of class society.

4. The formation and development of religion can only be explained by the historical conditions of production and existence.

5. In class society, generally speaking, the ruling and exploiting class always utilizes religion to anesthetize the people in order to maintain its rule. Religion serves the ruling class.

6. In history, the mass movements of the ruled often utilized religion. Under the cover of religion, they tried to reach the political and economic goals, but the ultimate effects of religion on such mass movements were negative.

7. The capitalist class utilized religion in its struggles against feudalism. Similarly, after becoming the ruling class, it utilizes religion to dupe the people and maintain its rule.

8. Christianity is a tool of colonialism and imperialism in invasion and expansion.

9. In medieval Europe, religion severely obstructed the development of science.

10. The extinction of religion is an inexorable law of social historical development but will go through a long and tortuous process.

In a 2008 article, Gong further updates his "comprehensive grasping and scientific evaluating Leninist view of religion."[19] Criticizing the opinions dismissing Lenin's view of religion among some Chinese Marxist theoreticians, Gong argues that Lenin enriched and developed the Marxist view of religion. According to Gong, Lenin's viewpoints should be taken as orthodox Marxism, which he summarizes as follows:

1. We must apply historical materialism to guide the research on religion and religious issues.
2. God in essence is a notion formed under the oppression of external forces.
3. The roots of religion in class society are in social classes.
4. Religion is a kind of spiritual tacky booze, a spiritual tool to maintain rule of the exploiting class.
5. The worldviews of scientific socialism and of religion absolutely cannot be reconciled.
6. Dealing with the religious problem must be subordinated to the overall mission of the socialist endeavor.
7. In the socialist movement, we should strive to unite the religious believers and progressive religious clergy.
8. We must struggle against the "left"-leaning mistakes in dealing with religious problems; we must handle religious problems carefully.
9. We must eliminate religious exploitation and privileges, separate church and state, separate church and school, and institute freedom of religious belief.
10. Religion is a private matter to the state but not a private matter to the workers' party. The Communists must adhere to atheism.
11. We must insist on atheist education for members of the party and the masses of the people.

By reviewing and explicating Marx, Engels, and Lenin, Gong reaffirms militant atheism as the Marxist orthodoxy. This form of atheism continues its pervasive influence among CCP officials through training classes at the CCP schools and also through other propaganda mechanisms. Gong's other book, *General Introduction to Religious Problems*, designated as "an official reading of the cadres," was first published in 1997 and has been updated and is in its third edition published in 2007. It was reportedly recommended by the CCP general secretary and president Jiang Zemin. The editorial preface says, "In April 1999, then CCP General Secretary Comrade Jiang Zemin came to Sichuan on an inspection tour, during which he talked many times about the importance of ethnic and religious issues, and the importance for the CCP members and officials to understand ethnicity and religion. On April 23, General Secretary Jiang once again stressed the importance for leading officials to study ethnicity and religion, and earnestly recommended two of the books published by our press," including this one.[20]

The impact of this kind of books on the minds of the Communist cadres is beyond doubt. During my research trips in China in the last decade, I have routinely heard government officials and CCP theoreticians of various ranks reiterate these viewpoints of militant atheism. Some of these people seem to have been exposed to no alternative views of religion in spite of the new "opium war" described above. If these rank-and-file CCP officials continue to dominate the decision making of religious affairs and policy, it will be difficult for any substantial change of the religious policy to occur.

On the other hand, religious research scholars decreasingly follow the Party line of atheism. While Gong, who studied as a graduate student under Lü Daji in the 1980s before taking the position at the CCP Central School, has stuck with the leftist position of militant atheism, Lü himself has shifted away from Marxist orthodoxy toward a value-free scientific approach to religion, as described above. Recently, Mou Zhongjian, a close friend and colleague of Lü, wrote an article entitled "The Chinese Socialists Ought to be Mild Atheists." He distinguishes three kinds of atheisms: faithless atheism, militant atheism, and mild atheism. He speaks against what he called the "faithless atheists," who believe in nothing but the fetishism of money; he insists that such people cannot be real socialists. He groups enlightenment and Bolshevik together as militant atheism, which is antireligious. The alternative is what he calls *wenhe wushenlun* (mild atheism). Mild atheists do not believe in religion but hold a rational attitude toward religion, which, Mou claims, is the authentic Marxist view of religion.

Mild atheism is deeper and better than other atheisms, Mou argues, as it sees the social and epistemological roots of theism and sees religious effects in human history. Therefore, Marxist atheism opposes declaring a war against religion but holds that we must gradually eliminate the alienating natural and social forces that oppress people through social reforms and development. It never aggravates the conflicts between theists and atheists, holds that they should respect each other, sincerely upholds freedom of belief, emphasizes solidarity between atheists and theists, and guides people to create heaven on earth. This atheism is the truly scientific atheism.[21]

Mou argues that this orthodox Marxist view of religion does not hold that scientific education will move people away from religion, as religion has deeper social and epistemological roots. Therefore, he opposes the "scientific atheism" propaganda currently fashionable in China, which, in Mou's view, is no different from the Leninist militant atheism and is destructive to social development. He says that mild atheists ought to hold firmly to socialist beliefs, respect religious faith, not claim to hold the whole truth of the universe in their own hands, and uphold cultural pluralism in modern society and protection of human rights. In 2010, Mou's mild atheism remained peripheral in the official discourse of the Chinese authorities.

CONCLUSION

The evolution of atheism and the debates surrounding the definition and essence of religion in China show the gradual change of mind among Chinese scholars and theoreticians, moving away from militant atheism toward an appreciation of certain positive values of religion. On the other hand, the theoretical discourse remains primarily within the narrow boundaries of Marxism, which the CCP insistently claims to be the guiding ideology for the Party and the state. Within the textual limits of the writings of Marx, Engels, Lenin, and Mao, some Chinese theoreticians and academicians have creatively justified the enlargement of religious tolerance, but its political bondage is firmly entrenched. This social and political reality stifles creative thinking and theoretical imagination among Chinese scholars of religion. Social-scientific theorizing and research remain underdeveloped in China today.

In the reform era, the relationship between the academy and the government regarding religion has become increasingly interactive. While the Party and the government still set limits and guidelines for academic research, scholars sometimes test these limits and push the boundaries. Some research projects have even made evident impacts on the adjustment of religious policy. An example is the research team of the Shanghai Academy of Social Sciences, which published its empirical research findings and a rereading of Marxist works in a book, *Religious Problems in the Era of Socialist China,* in 1987.[22] In this research, it is argued that religion and socialist society can be made compatible and that they should adapt to or accommodate each other. Upon publication, the book immediately stirred up debates. Some Marxist theoreticians wrote in opposition on the basis of atheism, but more scholars and theoreticians spoke in favor and support.[23] Eventually, in 1993, the authorities officially adopted the language of mutual adaptation, although with its own twists in policy application to actively guide religions to adapt to socialist society. Nowadays, the religious affairs officials proclaim the adaptation of religion and socialism as a mantra on almost all occasions. This makes possible the call for mild atheism by certain scholars. Apparently, religious research in China has emerged as the third force, besides that of the religious believers and the authorities, playing complicated but increasingly important roles in China's religious scene.

REGULATING RELIGION UNDER

COMMUNISM

DURING THE SIXTY years of Communist rule in China, the atheism-based regulation of religion has undergone some changes. Chronologically, it has had four distinct periods: (1) from 1949 to 1957, the Party-state[1] suppressed various religions and co-opted the five major religions through establishing the "patriotic" religious associations; (2) from 1957 to 1966, the socialist transformation was imposed to the "patriotic" religious groups and forcefully reduced the number of religious venues; (3) from 1966 to 1979, all religious venues were closed down, and religion was banned; and (4) from 1979 to 2009, limited tolerance of certain religious groups was governed by increasingly restrictive regulations. While the economy has undergone dramatic reforms toward a market economy, the religious policy and regulation have remained ideology-driven and have seen no substantial change from the pre-Cultural Revolution era. This religious policy, initially designed in the late 1950s, was intended for a totalitarian society with a centrally planned economy. In the new context of a market economy in an increasingly globalized society, the religious policy has become seriously outmoded, thus making inevitable its ineffectiveness in containing religion within the current social structure.

More detailed research is needed to clarify many of the specific developments in various periods, various parts of the country, various religions, and various departments or individual officials. For the purposes of this book, however, this chapter provides only a sketch of the historical changes and current tenets of the religious policy, sufficient as the contextual background for the theoretical explanations in the following chapters.

1949–1957: CO-OPTATION AND CONTROL

Soon after the founding of the People's Republic of China (PRC) in 1949, the Communist Party launched political campaigns against religious organizations as the ideological enemy and subversive political forces. First, the Party-state banned the cultic or heterodox sects of Chinese traditions. Hundreds of sectarian groups, including Yiguan Dao (I-Kuan Tao)[2] and numerous "redemptive societies," as they are called by some sinologists,[3] were considered antirevolutionary and reactionary *hui-dao-men* that had sided with the Guomindang (Kuomintang, Nationalist Party). Their leaders were rounded up, their organizations were broken down, and all of their activities were banned. Second, the Party-state adopted a more tactical and careful approach to the major religions, because these religions had massive numbers of followers, and most of them had international connections. Instead of following the ideological urge to eliminate religion immediately, the Party-state took pragmatic yet strategic measures to co-opt and control a select few leaders of the major religions and through the cooperative leaders coerced the religious groups and individuals to cut off their imperialist ties with the outside world and to cleanse feudalist elements from within.

In July 1950, under the supervision of the CCP United Front Department, a small group for investigating religious problems was established within the Commission of Culture and Education under the Government Administration Council. This "small group" was charged to investigate the religious situation and problems, especially with regard to Catholicism, Christianity (Protestantism), and Buddhism, and to propose policies and guiding principles to deal with these religions. Six months later, in January 1951, the "small group" became a formal Religious Affairs Department within the Commission of Culture and Education. By the end of 1952, the Religious Affairs Department (RAD) had been expanded to all provincial-level and most prefecture- and county-level governments.[4] The main tasks of the RADs during the first few years of the new China included driving out the foreign missionaries, pressing Catholics and Protestants to cut off ties completely with foreign countries, and handling the transition of the educational institutions, charity organizations, and religious bodies that at one point received funding or subsidies from the United States and other Western countries.

The co-optation and control strategy was first applied to Protestant Christians. The CCP hand-picked seven people as religious representatives to participate in the First National Political Consultative Conference (NPCC), which was held in September 1949, to bestow a form of legitimacy to the founding of the People's Republic of China. Wu Yaozong, a leader of the Young Men's Christian Association based in Shanghai, was designated the "chief representative" of the religious sector in the NPCC. The sector included three other Protestants, two Buddhists, and one Muslim as representatives and another Christian as the alternate representative. Wu was then instructed and entrusted to lead a "patriotic" movement for the Chinese Protestant churches to become self-ruling, self-supporting, and self-propagating; this later became known as the "Three-Selfs" principle. As part of the antiimperialism campaign in the early 1950s, Christian churches and organizations were required to sever foreign ties completely and immediately. The Party-state facilitated Wu and other Christian leaders to mobilize local churches to drive out foreign missionaries, reject financial support from missionary organizations, and cut off ties with the World Council of Churches and other international Christian organizations. The Christian schools, universities, and hospitals were either closed down or taken over by the government. The CCP leaders desired that Chinese Catholics enact the same three-self reforms. When these maneuvers were met with great resistances by the Catholic clergy, the Party-state responded with severe crackdowns on the clergy, expelling not only the representative of the Vatican in Nanjing but also foreign leaders of religious orders and foreign bishops. Some foreign missionaries and loyal Chinese Catholics were accused and prosecuted as spies of the United States or as antirevolutionary elements.

In the early years of the People's Republic of China, Buddhists among the Han majority seemed to be less a concern of the CCP leaders. But the antifeudalism campaigns included Buddhism, Daoism, and Islam as targets for revolutionary cleansing, with these campaigns insisting on both eliminating feudalist exploitation and reducing the power and influence of the varied clergy. Some of the Buddhist,

Daoist, and Muslim clergy were penalized either as landlords or as antirevolutionary and reactionary elements.

In 1954, after the State Council was organized according to the mandates of the first National People's Congress, the Religious Affairs Department was upgraded and expanded to become the Religious Affairs Bureau, directly reporting to the State Council. Within a year, the Religious Affairs Bureaus were strengthened throughout the provincial- and county-level governments (departments or offices). The handling of Islamic affairs remained the responsibility of the State Commission of Nationalities until 1957, when it was transferred to the Religious Affairs Bureau.

Under the guidance and supervision of the CCP United Front Department and the state's Religious Affairs Bureau (RAB), frequently involving the very highest of CCP leaders such as Premier Zhou Enlai, the Party-state maneuvered to form national associations for the five religions, namely the Buddhist Association of China (1953), the Islamic Association of China (1953), the Christian Three-Selfs Patriotic Movement Committee of China (1954), the Daoist Association of China (1957), and the Catholic Laity Patriotic Association of China (1957), which was renamed the Catholic Patriotic Association of China in 1962. Thereafter, these "patriotic" associations served as an integral part of the control mechanism of CCP religious policy.

1957–1966: THE SOCIALIST TRANSFORMATION

By 1957, the "socialist transformation" of the economy was essentially completed in the urban areas and accelerated in the rural areas. In the urban areas, all industrial and commercial companies were transformed into state-owned or collectively owned enterprises; urban residents were organized into work units and neighborhood committees. In the rural areas, farm lands and farmers were organized into socialist communes and production brigades. Beginning with the Second Five-Year Plan in 1958, central planning was imposed on the whole economy. In the new socialist society, the ideal principle of distribution of consumer materials was established as "from each according to his ability, to each according to his labor." Everyone in the country was supposed to participate in labor of material production. In light of this, the religious clergy were *fruges consumere nati* or parasites who contributed nothing but the poisonous opium of the people. For the purposes of economic production, therefore, the socialist transformation was carried out to reduce the clergy and reduce religious activities.

If the initial measures following the founding of the People's Republic were to eliminate the political threats of religious groups to the new social and political order, now the policy had been shifted to increasing economic production. At least in appearance, the CCP leadership seemed eager to increase production by all means, including converting the religious clergy into physical laborers. This was clearly uttered by Chairman Mao in regard to Tibetan Buddhism, but it was also applicable to other religions. The socialist transformation was postponed in the ethnic-minority regions until 1959, when the Dalai Lama led riots in Tibet, failed, and fled to safety in India. Within less than a month of the Lhasa riots and the Dalai Lama's departure, on April 15, 1959, Mao told the Supreme State Affairs Meeting that the Lama religion must be reformed: "There are 80,000 lamas in a population of 1,200,000 and these 80,000 lamas do not produce matter nor produce people....Lamas must engage in production, farming or industry."[5] In 1961, in a conversation with the Panchen Lama, who became the highest spiritual and secular leader of Tibetans after the Dalai Lama's exile, Mao reiterated this concern with some adjusted statistics: "In the past, among the 1,100,000 [Tibetan] people there were 110,000 lamas. This is too many, [we] can't feed them, and it's not good for developing production and population."[6]

For Muslims, the Socialist Transformation also resulted in institutional reform. On August 10, 1958, the United Front Department published a circular, "The Opinions regarding Religious Reformation among the Hui Nationality." In this circular, the Party stated that frequent and large-scale religious activities caused financial and labor wastes. Therefore, the religious activities of scripture reading and worshipping should be reduced, as they were a waste of time for work. While people may keep their beliefs, the religious institution must be reformed, stripping the power, property, and authority of the religious organizations. Religion and ethnicity must be separated, "so that a batch of Hui people without Islamic beliefs can emerge."[7] When some Muslim leaders resisted such reformations, they were exposed to "mass struggle meetings"[8] and penalized as the rightists or antirevolutionaries.

For Christians, the Socialist Transformation also led to disbanding denominations, converting professional ministers to physical laborers, and consolidating and reducing the numbers of churches and worship services. Regardless of previous denominational backgrounds, all Protestant Christians were amalgamated for joint worship services at the consolidated churches under the supervision of the local

Christian Three-Selfs Patriotic Movement Committee. The resistant leaders of Christian sects and independent congregations were imprisoned or sent to labor camps. The Chinese Protestant churches were forced into the so-called post-denominational era.

Indeed, this amalgamation was imposed on all five religions. Many temples, churches, and mosques were closed down or converted for nonreligious use. The ones that were left open for religious activities had to reduce the frequency of religious activities. A number of religious leaders, including Wu Yaozong, voiced their displeasure about these changes at the National Political Consultative Conference in spring 1957 and expressed their worries about the very existence of religion. However, by then, the five religions had been under effective control of the Party-state. Premier Zhou Enlai responded to the complaint on August 4, 1957, with these hard-hitting words: "Now you should not worry about whether religion can exist or not, but about whether the nation will prosper or not."[9] The antirightist campaign and the socialist education campaign soon muted all of the resistances. Religious sites and activities began diminishing in the following years. Some prefectures or counties were declared "no-religion prefectures" or "no-religion counties." Scholarly interviews and fieldwork research in recent years reveal that religious gatherings ceased by 1964 in various parts of the country.

1966–1979: ERADICATION

In 1966, Mao Zedong single-handedly launched the Great Proletarian Cultural Revolution to purge the "bourgeois elements" believed to be permeating the Party and society at large. To remove the feudalist, capitalist, and Soviet revisionist elements, Chairman Mao mobilized the youth, who formed Red Guard groups around the country. The Cultural Revolution began with the campaign to destroy and sweep away the "Four Olds": old customs, old culture, old habits, and old ideas. All religion fell into the categories of the Four Olds. Following Mao's call, Red Guards began to ransack traditional architectures, burn classic books and paintings, and shatter antiquities. As a result, many ancient cultural artifacts were destroyed.

The Red Guards' rampage shut down all existing religious venues throughout the country. Many buildings were actually torn apart, statues of gods and religious artifacts smashed, and religious scriptures burned. Some people took great risks to save scriptures, sculptures, and buildings in the name of preserving antiques or cultural heritage, but secretly keeping a religious scripture or an artifact was a crime and subject to mass struggles, labor camp, or imprisonment. Intellectuals, religious leaders, and staunch believers were targeted as personifications of the Four Olds, and many of them were mocked, harassed, imprisoned, tortured, or killed. The remaining believers were forced to make public renunciations and became subject to mass struggle meetings.

Having seen the eradication measures during the Cultural Revolution, many scholars in the West pronounced the death of religion in China.[10] However, as would become clear many years later, religion disappeared only from the public scene. Not only did many people maintain their faith in secret, but persevering believers also gathered for worship at home or in the wilderness. Religion simply went underground.

Interestingly, the centralization of power into the hands of Mao Zedong led to the personality cult of Mao. Mao was admired and worshipped in addition to being feared. There were the "red seas" of the "little red book" (*Quotations of Chairman Mao*) in Tiananmen Square and other municipal squares. Many people performed confession rituals in front of Mao's portrait or statue at the office or at home. There were daily rituals of reading Mao's books and extolling Mao at schools, factories, and farm edges.[11]

It is interesting that from the beginning of the People's Republic of China, the freedom of religious belief was inserted and preserved in the constitution. For instance, the 1949 temporary constitution of the "Common Program of the Chinese People's Political Consultative Conference" states that the citizens of the People's Republic of China have the freedom of religious belief. This was also adopted in the 1954 Constitution by the First National People's Congress. During the Cultural Revolution, the 1975 Constitution kept the clause of the freedom of religious belief but added the freedom of atheist propaganda. In practice, however, until today, the Constitution has never served as the basis of law under Communist rule.

1979–2010: STRENGTHENING THE REGULATION

Following the death of Mao in 1976, Deng Xiaoping gradually emerged as the paramount leader within the CCP. Under his leadership, the CCP set a new course for the country, focusing on modernization and economic development. In order to rally the Chinese people around the central task of economic development, the pragmatic CCP began to loosen control over various aspects of social life. Since the late 1950s,

CCP United Front Department head Li Weihan had proposed to grant tolerance of religion while insisting on atheist propaganda. But this tolerance policy, based on enlightenment atheism as described in chapter 3 above, was derailed by the increasingly leftist tendency of Mao and the radical CCP top leaders. Finally, under the pragmatic leadership of Deng, enlightenment atheism prevailed over militant atheism. Beginning in 1979, a limited number of Protestant and Catholic churches, Buddhist and Daoist temples, and Islamic mosques reopened for religious services.

In 1982, religious tolerance was formally inscribed in a new edict, "The Basic Viewpoint and Policy on the Religious Affairs during the Socialist Period of Our Country." It has become better known as Document No. 19. This central document has served as the basis for religious policy in China since that time. It grants legal existence to Buddhism, Daoism, Islam, Protestantism, and Catholicism under the government-sanctioned "patriotic" associations but not to any group outside of the five religious associations or to any other religions in the nation or the world at large. Furthermore, Document No. 19 proscribes proselytizing outside of approved religious premises and directs that atheist propaganda must be carried out unremittingly, just not inside religious venues. In line with Document No. 19, the PRC Constitution of 1982 reaffirms freedom of religious belief yet stipulates that only "normal" religious activities are protected. In practice, what is counted as "normal" is arbitrarily decided by the administrators in position at the time, especially those of the United Front Department, the Religious Affairs Bureau, and the Public Security Bureau.

Since 1982, the Party-state has promulgated circulars, enacted ordinances, and issued administrative orders[12] that

have increasingly tightened control over religious organizations. For example, in 1991, the CCP issued Document No. 6,
which calls for strengthening the religious affairs administration, including an expansion of the number of Religious
Affairs Bureau (RAB) cadres down to the township level of
government. In 1994, the State Council published two ordinances that require all religious groups to register with the
government and prohibit foreigners from proselytizing in
China. In 1996, the CCP and the State Council issued a joint
decree to curb the building of temples and outdoor Buddha
statues and to constrict authority to grant new building per-
mits for religious venues to provincial governments. In 1999,
Falun Gong was banned as an "evil cult" (*xie jiao*), and its core
leaders were jailed, although the movement's founder took
refuge in the United States. After the initial crackdown on
Falun Gong, the National People's Congress Standing
Committee adopted a "Legislative Resolution on Banning
Heretical Cults" in October 1999, which presented a form of
legitimacy to the crackdown on Falun Gong and other *qigong*
or cultic groups. In the following years, provincial governments issued numerous "temporary" or "draft" ordinances and
administrative orders aimed at controlling religious groups.
Eventually, these administrative orders were consolidated into
the State Council's Regulations of Religious Affairs, which took
effect on March 1, 2005. Since the collapse of the Soviet bloc in
the early 1990s, the antiinfiltration of foreign missionaries has
become a key focus in religious policy.

Once the total ban of religion was lifted in 1979, however, a religious upsurge outpaced regulatory expansion in
spite of accelerated efforts at control. Economic development
remains the central task of CCP top leadership. Many local
governments have often used this to justify the pragmatic

and tolerant approach to various religions. In other words, while the party's United Front Department and the state's RAB put antiinfiltration as the highest priority, many other governmental agencies have tried to put religion to use for economic development, such as building temples for tourism or allowing for more churches in order to attract overseas investments. In the reform era, the economic consideration often prevails, which exacerbates the frustrations of religious affairs cadres over the loss of control.

Recently, instead of equally repressing all religions, the regime has taken cautious steps to promote Buddhism, Daoism, folk religions, and Confucianism, in part to counter the rapid increase of Christianity. The China Religious Culture Communication Association (CRCCA), working in the shadow of the State Administration for Religious Affairs (SARA), organized the first World Buddhist Forum in 2006, the second one in March 2009, and the International Daodejing[13] Forum in 2007. Yet neither SARA nor CRCCA has announced any plan to organize or grant permission for similar forums about Christianity or Islam. Not surprisingly, many Buddhist and Daoist leaders and believers are not hesitant to proclaim that "this is the best time of religious freedom in the entire history of China."

The current policy's favoritism toward Buddhism and Daoism does not have a theoretical justification based on Marxism, which is still nominally the CCP orthodox ideology. In 2010, it appeared that different factions of the CCP leadership had engaged in discussions about reforming the religious policy. Some traditionalists have called for adopting measures of the Chinese imperial dynasties to control religious and ethnic minorities and oppose foreign religions. Some liberals advocate for adjusting the religious regulation according to international conventions and granting greater freedom and equality to the varied religious groups. Yet the pragmatic conservatives seem to want to maintain the status quo.

THE CONTROL APPARATUS

Document No. 19 insists that atheism is a basic doctrine of the Chinese Communist Party and that the whole Party and state are responsible for implementing the religious policy. Part 12 of Document No. 19 specifically lists these relevant agencies, "including the united front department, the religious affairs bureau, the nationalities affairs commission, the political-legal ministry, the ministries of propaganda, culture, education, science and technology, and health, and the people's associations of the Workers' Union, the Communist Youth League, and the Women's Union."[14] Apparently, the control apparatus is all-encompassing. The circular stresses the importance for all of these departments to "seek unity of thinking, unity of cognition, and unity of policy, divide work with responsibility, act in close coordination, take this important work into hands earnestly, and do it persistently and seriously." It demands that the Party theoreticians and propaganda cadres must realize that applying the Marxist position, view, and method to religious research and propagating atheism to the people are important components of the CCP's work.

Regarding the division of work and responsibility, the major control apparatus includes the United Front Department of the CCP and the Religious Affairs Bureau of the government. The United Front Department of the CCP Central Committee has a division of religious and ethnic affairs, which is charged both to make religious policies and to rally religious leaders around the CCP. The day-to-day administration of religious affairs lies in the Religious Affairs Bureau of the State Council. The RAB is sometimes combined with the Commission of Nationalities Affairs at the provincial and county levels, and the provincial- and lower-level RAB chief is often an associate director of the CCP's United Front Department at the corresponding level.

Since the restoration of the Religious Affairs Bureau of the State Council in 1979, significant increases in religious affairs cadres have happened in 1988, 1994, 1998, and 2004. By the end of 1995, there were 3,053 religious affairs officials on the county level or above. Meanwhile, more functions have been added to the RAB of the State Council, including the Research Center of Religion in 1988 and the publisher of *China Religion* magazine and the Religious Culture Press in 1994. In 1998, the RAB of the State Council was renamed the State Administration of Religious Affairs (SARA), with increased administrative status within the central government system. SARA's main responsibilities, as published on government Web sites, include the powers to:

- investigate and suggest guiding principles and policies for religious affairs;
- administrate and supervise the implementation and enforcement of laws, regulations, and policies on religion;
- formulate measures and organize the implementation of religious policies;
- investigate the religious situation and trends inside and outside China;
- conduct research on theories of religious issues;
- draft laws and regulations on religion;

- protect the policy of the citizens' freedom of religious belief according to law;
- protect the rights of the religious organizations and venues according to law;
- protect the normal liturgical activities of the religious clergy;
- protect the normal religious activities of the believers;
- prevent illegal activities in the name of religion;
- promote education in patriotism and socialism and support the unification of the motherland and ethnic unity among religious people;
- solidify and strengthen the patriotic united front of the religious people;
- unite and mobilize the vast number of religious believers to serve the reforms and opening and economic construction;
- help religious bodies to educate religious clergy through religious schools;
- facilitate religious bodies in their dealing with various government agencies;
- organize and guide the propaganda of religious policies and regulations;
- guide local government's religious affairs departments;
- assist local governments in handling religious problems in a timely manner; and
- support and help religious exchanges with other countries and with Hong Kong, Macau, and Taiwan.

In short, SARA oversees and manages day-to-day religion-related affairs, including processing requests for approving the opening of temples, churches, and mosques; approving special religious gatherings and activities; and approving the appointment of leaders of religious associations. Besides the UFD and the RAB, religious associations must also register with the Ministry of Civil Affairs, but the registration must be stamped first by the RAB.

Meanwhile, the Ministry of Public Security (police) deals with all illegal religious activities, including any illegal activities of the five official religions and all activities of all other religions. The Ministry of State Security also watches over some religious groups and active leaders, especially since the early 1990s, when the Chinese authorities intensified the fight against infiltration by foreign religious organizations and foreign political entities using religion. Since the crackdown on Falun Gong and the banning of "evil cults," more resources have been put into religious control and atheist propaganda, including publishing the new magazine *Science and Atheism* and books about atheism, organizing atheist and anticult associations, organizing atheist and anticult exhibitions, and organizing study sessions by the CCP and Communist Youth League branches. An anticult ministry has been developed under the code name of the "610 Office" (it is said that the name came from the CCP directive on June 10, 1999, that established this anticult ministry). The 610 Office at the top level has a higher status than the State Administration of Religious Affairs. A 610 Office has been added to provincial-, prefecture-, and even county-level governments.

In practice, the SARA and lower-level RABs usually rule through the so-called patriotic religious associations. The associations of the five official religions are nongovernmental organizations in name, but they function as an extension and delegation of the RAB. For example, in principle, the provincial-level Three-Self Patriotic Movement Committee (TSPM) holds the power of approval to ordain ministers, but no one can be ordained without prior approval by the provincial RAB. The prefecture- or county-level TSPM appoints the senior pastors of local churches, but the appointment must first be approved by the same-level RAB. More important, the national-, provincial-, prefecture-, and county-level TSPMs are separate organizations independent of one another. That is, the local TSPMs are not under the leadership of the provincial or national TSPMs. TSPMs report to the RAB on the same level and the one immediately above. When a church plans to organize meetings or activities involving people beyond the local administrative region, it has to apply to the higher-level RAB. That is, if the activity involves people from another county, it has to be approved by the prefecture RAB; if from another prefecture, then from the provincial RAB; if from another province or from another country, then from the SARA. These rules and mechanisms apply to all five religions.

CONCLUSION

Since the founding of the People's Republic of China, the religious policy has undergone four distinct periods. In the first period of 1949 to 1957, the policy focused on the political control of religious groups. The Party-state banned sectarian religions and co-opted five major religions into "patriotic" associations. In the second period of 1957 to 1966, the policy was centered on increasing economic productivity under central planning. The Socialist Transformation forced religions to disband denominations; stripped the power, property, and influence of the clergy; and reduced religious venues and worship gatherings. In the third period of 1966 to 1979, all churches, temples, and mosques were closed; religion was banned; and atheist education and propaganda were carried out throughout the country. Since 1979, the policy has allowed limited tolerance of religion under increasingly tightened regulations.

However, in the reform era since 1979, all kinds of religions have revived and are thriving. Christianity has been the fastest-growing religion for decades. Many Buddhist and Daoist temples have been restored. The state even sponsors large Buddhist gatherings and ceremonies to venerate Confucius and legendary ancestors of the Chinese people. In some areas, traditional Chinese temples have sprung up like mushrooms. Colorfully dressed people doing slow-motion exercises in unison became ubiquitous in public parks throughout the country in the 1980s and 1990s, but now such quasi-religious *qigong* practices have become rare. The personality cult of Communist leader Chairman Mao had its heyday during the Cultural Revolution, while at present, the worship of Mao has taken the form of folk religion, with dedicated temples and burning of incense sticks. All the while, the authorities have carried out waves of atheist propaganda, antisuperstition campaigns, and brutal crackdowns on underground Christian churches and various "evil cults."

There have been some adjustments in the implementation of the religious policy. Since the mid-1990s, the central and provincial governments have installed numerous administrative ordinances, climaxing in the Regulations on Religious Affairs decreed by the State Council, which became effective on March 1, 2005. But there have been no substantial deviations from the basic policy established in Document No. 19. There is a broad consensus among China observers and scholars who have closely followed these developments that China's religious policy remains strict.[15]

Religious regulation is a very important dimension of the religious scene, as the policy dominates and the religions have to respond to it. However, religious groups are by no means merely passive. The changing interactions between the authorities and religions have often led to consequences beyond control of the state. For example, the CCP effort to eradicate religion during the Cultural Revolution failed; the co-opting and control tactics initiated in the 1950s became increasingly ineffective in the reform era. The religious policy needs to respond and adapt to the changing reality, but the CCP theoreticians have not been prepared to see or understand the religious resurgence and continual growth.

During the reform era since the late 1970s, when many social spheres have undergone profound changes, the religious policy has remained the most ideologically driven sphere. It has become outmoded and lagged far behind the reality. The social reality is the emerging market economy in the increasingly globalized society, yet the religious policy was initiated around 1957–58, when China was just beginning to experiment with the central-planning economy in a totalitarian society. To apply Marxist terms, the superstructure, which includes ideology, has become incompatible with the economic basis today. The result is that the outdated religious policy has rendered itself ineffective in controlling religion, all the while antagonizing the Chinese populace and the world community. The religious policy has become one of the liabilities in China's stride for modernization and for entering the global stage. If the restrictive regulation persists in the current form of constraints and suppression, I would not be surprised if the religious policy becomes the last straw that breaks the camel's back.

THE RED, BLACK, AND GRAY

MARKETS OF RELIGION

RELIGION HAS BEEN reviving in China despite restrictive regulations imposed by the Chinese Communist Party (CCP). That religion can survive and thrive under atheist Communist rule raises important theoretical and practical questions: How much can the state control religious increases or decreases? How much can a secularist state promote secularization? Why did the eradication measures fail? If heavy regulation is not effective in reducing religious participation, what are the causes and consequences? This chapter provides a theoretical explanation of why the heavy regulation of religion will lead not to religious demise but, rather, to complication—it will result in a tripartite religious market with different dynamics.

DEFINITIONS AND PROPOSITIONS

All countries under Communist rule, past and present, have enacted harsh regulations against religion. Suppressive regulation may lead to the decline of one form of religiosity—participation in formal organizations—but other forms of religiosity, including beliefs and noninstitutionalized practices, are more difficult to control. When the restrictions are strict, some religious activities will go underground, and others will operate in the ambiguous gray areas. This is to say, the heavily regulated religious market may be divided into the red, black, and gray markets of religion.

Definition 1 A red market of religion consists of all legal (officially permitted) religious organizations, believers, and religious activities.

Alternatively, this may be called the "open market," because the religious exchanges are carried out openly. However, the market is not equally open to all religious groups. Moreover, the officially sanctioned religious organizations in this open market have to comply with the commands and orders of the political authorities. In Communist-ruled societies, the open market is stained "red," that is, colored with the official Communist ideology. The red stain is reflected in the rhetoric of the clergy, theological discourses, and practices. For example, the authorities require the clergy to teach believers to "love the country and love the religion" (*aiguo aijiao*), where loving the country precedes loving the religion. Moreover, loving the country is taken as synonymous with loving the Communist Party. This is a mantra that the clergy in the approved religious organizations must chant to gain legitimacy in the eyes of the authorities.[1] Some religious leaders also proclaim that the Communist utopian society is an ideal shared by the religion, so that religious believers should align themselves with the Communist Party in the Communist endeavor.[2] The open market in other monopoly and oligopoly economies is also constrained by political authorities, although the stain may have a different color or hue.

Definition 2 A black market of religion consists of all illegal (officially banned) religious organizations, believers, and religious activities.

The black-market exchanges are conducted underground or in secret. It is illegal, nonetheless it exists and operates, although only in the underground.

Definition 3 A gray market of religion consists of all religious and spiritual organizations, practitioners, and activities with ambiguous legal status.

These groups, individuals, and activities fall into a gray, ambiguous area of religious regulation. They can be perceived as both legal and illegal or neither legal nor illegal. Either there is a lack of explicit regulation on particular practices and organizations, or the kind of religious practices and organizations could be considered legal in terms of nonreligious regulations. The gray market is the most difficult to demarcate because of its ambiguous and amorphous nature. Broadly speaking, it includes two types of practices: (1) illegal religious activities of legally existing religious groups and (2) religious or spiritual practices that are manifested in culture or science instead of in religion.

Type 1 religious practices are conducted by legal religious suppliers and consumers evading restrictive regulation. For example, a regulation may prohibit proselytizing outside of religious premises and to children. Defying the regulation, family members and friends of an otherwise legal sect might gather at home to discuss their beliefs and in the process socialize their children into the religious faith. Further, religious groups and individuals may provide social services with the implicit intention to proselytize. Regulating these kinds of activities requires more elaborative rules regarding legal boundaries, and in enforcing such rules, authorities must exert great care to delineate ambiguous boundaries or borderline zones. Meanwhile, religious suppliers and consumers can be very creative in responding to adverse rules, making the enforcement of regulation costly and elusive. Creativity in evading regulations also makes it difficult for researchers to document and quantify the extent of gray-market religiosity.

Type 2 religious activities include various forms of informal or implicit religion and spirituality. These activities have been studied by scholars as folk religion, popular religion, primal religion, quasi-religion, New Age, occults, magic, yoga, client and audience cults, and/or new spiritualities.[3] Not all scholars agree that each of these activities should be classified as religious, but sociologists of religion generally agree that, regardless of the classification, spiritual alternatives compete for adherents with conventional religions. While it is difficult for scholars to define alternative spirituality, it is almost impossible for authorities to regulate it. Rather than professing specific religious beliefs, alternative spiritualists may insist that their practices are culturally or scientifically based. For example, shamanism may be practiced as ethnic or folk dances, and spiritual healing might be carried out in the name of an alternative medicine. As culture or science, such activities arguably fall outside the boundaries of religious regulation. However, authorities may nevertheless try to bring such practices under control, especially when the supernatural elements of the beliefs or religious dimensions of the practices become more obvious. In short, as part of the gray market, informal spiritual practices are a constant challenge to regulators and researchers alike.

While several propositions about the triple markets of religion may be developed, three of them are central for understanding the general dynamics of religious change.

Proposition 1 To the extent that religious organizations are restricted in number and in operation, a black market of religion will emerge in spite of high costs to individuals.

The black market is a logical consequence of heavy regulation. Inasmuch as authorities restrict religion by sanctioning certain religious groups and activities, a regulation simultaneously makes other religious groups illegal. The intention of such regulation is to eliminate illegal groups and activities. In spite of regulation, history recounts multitudes of devout believers or what Max Weber called religious "virtuosos,"[4] who will seek and practice proscribed religions regardless of circumstance, in a clandestine manner if necessary. There are always people who are willing to pay a higher price for their religion, even to the extent of life sacrifice. When the state bans certain religious exchanges to the extent that the religious needs of certain market niches are not met within the open market, a black market will emerge to compensate.

Virtuosos aside, a population's religious needs cannot be unmet for an extended period of time. Consciously or unconsciously, people tend to express religious feelings and consume religious goods. For example, during China's Cultural Revolution (1966–1976), when all religious organizations were banned and quasi-religious practices were suppressed, the religious zeal of the masses found an improbable outlet: the Mao personality cult or the broad "political religion,"[5] which is a form of pseudo-religion as defined in chapter 2 above. In post-Mao China, the semireligious *qigong* replaced Maoism as an outlet for religious zealotry.

Proposition 2 To the extent that a red market of religion is restricted and a black market of religion is suppressed, a gray market of religion will emerge.

The risks and costs of black-market religion are high because of government measures. At the same time, red-market religious groups under heavy regulation are limited in number and inaccessible for many people. Moreover, approved religious groups are commonly red-stained because of the restrictions imposed by political authorities, which often result in "sanitized" or "watered-down" religious goods and services.[6] When people cannot find satisfaction in the red market and are unwilling to risk black-market penalties, a gray market fills the gap or the niche. In the gray market, individuals resort to informal religious practices and spiritual alternatives, such as Mao worship or *qigong*, as will be explained below. Alternatively, legally existing groups evade regulation by offering illegal religious services.

Proposition 3 The more restrictive and suppressive the regulation, the larger the gray market of religion necessarily becomes.

The relative size of each of the triple markets largely depends on both the severity of regulation and the effectiveness of enforcement. In a minimally regulated economy, like that of the United States, the open market can meet the religious needs of most people. In a heavily regulated economy, the high-cost black market draws only a small number of staunch believers, and the red market is either inaccessible or unappealing to large numbers of people. Unable or unwilling to engage in either the open market or the black market, many people resort to the gray market to meet their religious needs, resulting in a proportionally expanded gray market.

Proposition 3 may appear counterintuitive. Unrelenting atheist education in Communist-ruled societies appears to have reduced the need for religion in the populace. However, the rebound of religiosity in almost all post-Soviet societies shows that the artificial reduction in religious need was mostly illusory or temporary at best.[7] Some professed atheists during the Soviet period were discreet religious believers.[8] Perhaps more people practiced alternative forms of gray-market spirituality, such as popular religion, shamanism, or the personality cult of Lenin, as a substitute for "real" religion.[9] In China during the Cultural Revolution, the red market did not exist, the black market was severely suppressed, and most forms of gray-market religion—popular religion and alternative spiritualities—were also repressed. However, one form of gray-market religion reached its peak during this period. The Mao personality cult or "political religion" had hundreds of millions of sincere worshippers. Communist Party Chairman Mao was glorified as "the great savior of the people" (*renmin de da jiuxing*) and "the Red Sun" (*hong taiyang*). People danced and sang to Mao's statue and confessed sins and made vows before Mao's portrait.[10] The "Little Red Book" of Mao's words was revered. Studying Mao's quotes was institutionalized into the daily schedule of government officials, students, factory workers, and farmers. Even mathematics and science lessons in all textbooks began with the words of Chairman Mao.

To summarize these propositions in dynamic terms, increased religious regulation will lead not to a reduction of religion per se but to the triple religious market. Although participation in formal religious organizations may decline, other forms of religiosity will persist and tend to increase. Moreover, given its ambiguous nature, a gray market in a heavily regulated society is likely to be large, volatile, and unsettled, making religious regulation an arduous task and impossible to enforce. Let us now examine each of the three markets in China under Communist rule.

THE RED MARKET

Since 1949, except for the thirteen radical years between 1966 and 1979, the Chinese government has granted legal status to five religions under the control of "patriotic" associations: Buddhism, Daoism, Islam, Protestantism, and Catholicism. Chinese government sources have provided some religious statistics, as shown in table 5.1. The sources vary from officially released white papers to the authoritative Xinhua News releases to statements by top leaders. Although these official sources are not consistent with one another, nor are they precise, they nonetheless provide ballpark estimates of the red-market religion.

Some caveats are necessary regarding these numbers from the Chinese authorities. First of all, these estimates are commonly regarded as guesses at best and fabricated at worst. The only certainty is that they are serious undercounts of the actual numbers of believers. Because of the Communist desire for reducing religion, local government officials tend to report lower numbers of religious believers than what actually exist

Table 5.1

OFFICIAL STATISTICS OF FIVE RELIGIONS IN CHINA

	Catholic	Protestant	Islamic	Buddhist	Daoist
	Believers (million)	Believers (million)	Population[1] (million)	Believers (million)	Believers (million)
Early 1950s[a]	2.7	0.7	8.0		
1956[b]	3.0	0.8	10.0	Several tens of millions[3]	10.0[3]
1982[a]	3.0	3.0	10.0		
1991[c]	3.5	4.5	17.0		
1995[d]	4.0	10.0	18.0		
2009[e]	5.3	16.0	21.0		
	Clergy[4]	Clergy[4]	Clergy[4]	Monks/Nuns[4]	Monks/Nuns[4]
1982[a]	3,400	5,900	20,000	27,000	2,600
1995[d]	4,300	18,000	40,000	200,000	25,700
2009[e]	5,260	37,000	40,000	200,000	50,000

(continued)

Table 5.1

(continued)

| | Catholic | Protestant | Islamic | Buddhist | Daoist |
	Churches and meeting points[5]	Churches and meeting points[5]	Mosques[5]	Temples[5]	Temples[5]
1995[d]	4,377	37,000	36,200	13,000	1,557
2009[e]	6,000	58,000	35,000	20,000	3,000

Sources: a. Document No. 19, "The Basic Viewpoint and Policy on the Religious Affairs during the Socialist Period of Our Country." For a translation of and commentary on this CCP circular, see MacInnis, *Religion in China Today*.
b. Luo,[1] *1949–1999*. Luo was an official of the CCP United Front Department.
c. Information Office of the PRC State Council, *White Paper on the Status of Human Rights in China* (Beijing: Information Office of the PRC State Council, 1991).
d. Li Pingye,[1] *90 Niandai zhongguo zongjiao fazhan zhuangkuang baogao*" ("A Report of the Status of Religious Development in China in the 1990s"), *Journal of Christian Culture 2* (1999): 201–222. Li was an official of the CCP United Front Department.
e. Xinhua News Agency, "The Great Practice of the Freedom of Religious Belief: A Summary of the 60 Year's Religious Affairs since the Establishment of New China," September 4, 2009. It also states: "China now has more than a hundred million believers of various religions. The number of believers has been growing steadily. There are about 130,000 religious venues, increased about 50,000 than in 1997. Religious clergy and professionals are about 360,000, increased about 60,000 than in 1997. There are nearly 5,500 religious associations and over 110 religious schools" (http://news.xinhuanet.com/politics/2009-09/04/content_11997424.htm).

Notes: 1. The number of Muslims is the total population of ten ethnic minorities that consider Islam as their ethnic religion, although many do not practice or believe.

2. The number of the early 1950s are consistent with nongovernmental and non-Chinese publications.

3. No number of Buddhist and Daoist believers is given in most of the years, because there is no membership system. The only estimates in 1956 were uttered by Chairman Mao Zedong in a published conversation and reported in the book compiled by Luo Guangwu, as noted above.

4. The professional clergies of different religions are not totally comparable, because Buddhist and Daoist monks and nuns in certain orders may not interact with lay believers, whereas Catholic priests, Protestant pastors, and Islamic imams minister to the laity. Certain Catholic orders, such as the Trappists, may not interact with the laity, either, but such religious orders are not allowed to exist in China.

5. The religious venues of different religions also have very different functions: churches and mosques are buildings for regular weekly lay gathering, whereas many temples are monasteries in the mountains that receive occasional pilgrims, and some of them are secluded for hermits, with few or no outside visitors. The Protestant and Catholic "meeting points" are mostly congregations with simple, shabby buildings, not necessarily small congregations.

in the city or county. As a matter of fact, Ye Xiaowen, the head of the State Administration of Religious Affairs from 1995 to 2009, acknowledged this ubiquitous problem in a speech at the CCP Central School in Beijing. According to him, a major problem of gathering accurate statistics is that, as a rule of the political game, "the numbers come from the cadres; and the cadres come from the numbers. More precisely, regarding religion, it is 'the negative numbers come from the cadres; and the cadres come from the negative numbers.'"[11] In other words, local officials who report a negative growth or lower growth of religion are more likely to get promoted. But this is not simply a problem of the lower-rank governments or the officials. The State Administration of Religious Affairs itself has maintained in its official statements, from the mid-1990s until now, that "there are about a hundred million believers of all religions in China." In fact, this has been the officially sanctioned uniform statement about religious believers by all government officials or Party-state agencies. The 2009 Xinhua News Agency still said, "China now has more than a hundred million believers of various religions," even though it also admitted that "The number of believers has been growing steadily."[12]

Second, counting the actual number of religious believers within China is difficult. Neither Buddhism nor Daoism has a membership system. A Buddhist or Daoist believer does not *belong* to a particular temple, may patronize several temples or masters, or may practice at home. Moreover, although Protestant and Catholic churches have had clear definitions of membership, congregational leaders are often discouraged from reporting the actual number of church members because of the government's hostile policies toward religion. Many churches, as a measure of safeguarding the believers, do not even keep baptismal records, so that baptized Christians are not easily identifiable by the authorities.

Nonetheless, the numbers reported by the Chinese authorities show some clear patterns. The numbers of believers listed for 1956 and 1982 in table 5.1 deserve particular attention. The 1956 numbers are the last official count before the coerced disbanding of denominations in 1957. After many years of severe suppression and thirteen years of eradication efforts (1966–1979), the official count published in 1982 indicates that the numbers of Catholics and Muslims remained about the same, while the number of Protestant Christians increased 3.75 times, from 800,000 to 3,000,000. Still, the actual increase of Christians could be even more pronounced than these reported numbers.

Of course, suppression has made dents. For one thing, open participation in formal religious organizations was reduced after 1957, decreased to zero during the Cultural Revolution, and remained low in proportion to the population through the 1980s. Since the mid-1990s, the authorities have repeatedly claimed that there are about 100 million religious believers. If this is so, the proportion of believers in the entire population is less than 9 percent (100 million out of 1.3 billion). If this low proportion is even remotely close to reality, people who wish for the demise of religion certainly have a good reason to celebrate, which indeed was marked as a partial victory of the atheist propaganda in the Document No. 19, as described in chapter 4 above. But the reality is not so simple. The 100 million religious believers can be only those within sight of the authorities, making up, in essence, the red market of religion. Many religious people have stayed away from the open practices in the red market but have engaged in the black and gray markets without acknowledgment by the state.

The open religious market is not a free market. Many restrictions are imposed on government-sanctioned churches, temples, and mosques. These include "monitoring by the state, required political study for pastors, certain restrictions on acceptable topics for preaching and intervention in church personnel matters."[13] Some restrictions are explicit in law, others are implicit in CCP circulars, and many are arbitrarily decided by local officials. Explicitly, Article 36 of the Constitution of the People's Republic of China, in effect since 1982, maintains: "The state protects normal religious activities. No one may make use of religion to engage in activities that disrupt public order, impair the health of citizens, or interfere with the educational system of the state." A key word here is "normal." Normal religious activities are defined by the officials in charge. What is normal in other countries may not be regarded normal in the eyes of the Chinese authorities. For example, religious education of children is a common practice in almost all countries. Until recently, however, providing religious education to children younger than eighteen has been prohibited to a great extent by the Chinese authorities. Christian churches could not lawfully hold Sunday school for children. In 2001, some Christians filed a lawsuit against the local RAB in Wenzhou, Zhejiang, contending for equal rights to comparable religious practice for their children.[14] After that, while the ban seems to be still in place, the RAB officials in many localities have turned a blind eye. Similarly, churches are not allowed to baptize children younger than eighteen. In some Muslim regions, sometimes children younger than eighteen are not allowed to enter the mosque. Of course, exceptions can be made when politically necessary, such as when a child was recognized as the reincarnation of the Tibetan Buddhist Panchen Lama. Religious initiation and education have been allowed for several boy lamas. In the red market of religion, the religious regulations are enforced inconsistently across different religions and different regions of the country. The authorities do not treat all officially allowed religions equally.

THE BLACK MARKET

When existing churches and temples cannot meet religious needs, many people will seek alternatives. Indeed, the black market of religion was initially created by the regime's anti-religious policy in the 1950s, when the government took great efforts to create the national "patriotic" religious associations. Many believers who refused to join them because of theological and political considerations simply went underground.

A major segment of the black market contains underground Catholics. The animosity between the Roman Catholic church and the CCP goes back to the founding of the PRC in 1949. According to sociologist Richard Madsen: "In 1949, the Vatican, led by the strongly anti-communist Pope Pius XII, forbade Chinese Catholics, under pain of excommunication, to co-operate in any way with the new Chinese regime.... Because of the Vatican's strict stance against any cooperation with communism, however, it was particularly difficult to find any Catholic bishops or priests who would accept leadership positions within the CPA [Catholic Patriotic Association]. Indeed, one requirement of accepting such a position was to sever one's allegiance to the Vatican, which for Catholics would have been seen as a major betrayal of their identity."[15]

For several years, the CCP authorities received little cooperation from the Catholic clergy. After persistent and heavy-handed maneuvers, the authorities eventually succeeded in establishing the "China Catholic Laypeople Patriotic Association" (*Zhongguo Tianzhu Jiaoyou Aiguohui*) in 1957.[16] Only after sentencing the most prominent Catholic leaders, such as Archbishop Ignatius Gong Pinmei of Shanghai,[17] to long prison terms did the authorities find five bishops willing to assume leadership roles within the patriotic association. Then these bishops went on to consecrate several other bishops without Vatican approval in 1957. "Most Catholics," however, "both clergy and laity, refused to participate in institutions controlled by these bishops. They carried on their faith in secret, sometimes under threat of severe punishment."[18]

Today, the underground Catholic church is well organized. An underground Catholic Bishops Conference operates parallel to the officially sanctioned "China Catholic Bishops Conference" within the China Catholic Patriotic Association.[19] Recent estimates put the total number of Catholics in China at 12 million.[20] About 4 million or 5 million are associated with the officially sanctioned Catholic church. "Perhaps six to eight million Catholics are associated with the so-called 'underground church.'"[21] In other words, until recently, about two-thirds of Catholics had been in the black market of religion.

Initially, Protestant Christians, including the Little Flock, the True Jesus Church, other sectarian groups, and some independent congregations, refused to join the Protestant Three-Self Patriotic Movement Committee (TSPM). Once again, the authorities responded by jailing the stubborn leaders. The best known among these individuals were Wang

Mingdao in Beijing and Watchman Nee in Shanghai. Subsequently, large numbers of Protestants agreed to join the TSPM. In 1957, however, many of them reversed course when, as dictated by the authorities, the TSPM Committee coerced all believers into the union worship service. All Protestants—Episcopalians, Methodists, Baptists, and sectarian members—were forced to disband their denominations and come together for unified worship. All church properties were centralized under the TSPM Committee. As a reaction, many Christians, especially those of sectarian backgrounds, completely stopped attending church under the TSPM. However, as devout believers, they would not stop gathering for worship. They simply resorted to gatherings at private homes or in the wilderness. In 2002, during my fieldwork research in Wenzhou, a coastal city in the southeast, a Christian leader pointed out to me the wooded hillside where, during the Cultural Revolution, they gathered for worship at night. While they were gathering, a watchman would stand guard at the foot of the hill. If police or militia security personnel came in sight, he would use a flashlight to signal imminent danger, and the congregation would scatter into the woods. They never stopped worship gatherings, according to this lay leader. Christians in many other regions similarly practiced in secrecy. These underground "house churches" became seeds of revivals in the 1980s and 1990s.[22]

Although many churches have reopened since 1979 under the auspices of TSPM, many house churches continue to stay underground. Dissenters criticize the TSPM mostly for its political submission to the authorities and also for the liberal theology among the TSPM top leaders. Moreover, as evangelical Christians, they cannot abide by the regulation that prohibits evangelism outside of church premises.

Because their existence and activities are illegal, the house churches "are vulnerable to much more coercive and punitive state action, including physical harassment, detention, fines, and labor re-education or criminal proceedings and prison sentences."[23] However, house churches are too widespread for the government to eliminate efficiently. Nonetheless, the Chinese authorities have singled out about twenty "evil cults" that sprang from Christianity and are active in more than one province, and they have taken resolute measures against them, including hunting down and jailing leaders and the most active members, tearing down their buildings, confiscating their possessions, and fining and reeducating (deprogramming) loyal followers. Table 5.2 provides a partial list of such Christianity-related sectarian groups that have been banned by the government. Not included in the table are many banned Protestant congregations and groups active within only one province, which may or may not be made known to the broader public.

Indeed, the rapid growth of underground churches in the countryside, coupled with a lack of orthodox theological training, has "resulted in some extreme groups evolving into sects which most Christians would unhesitatingly label heretical. Groups such as the *Beili wang* (Established king), *Mentuhui* (Disciples sect), and many others often have a charismatic leader who proclaims himself to be Christ or otherwise divine, and who creates new sacred instructions or scriptures."[24] However, many Christians outside of mainland China perceive some of the banned sectarian groups to be orthodox and evangelical. Some of their practices may be radical or extreme, such as covering heads in prayer or crying out as a required sign of real confession and conversion. However, in theology, they are not necessarily heretical.

Table 5.2

A PARTIAL LIST OF INDIGENOUS, CHRISTIANITY-RELATED SECTARIAN OR CULTIC GROUPS THAT HAD SPREAD ACROSS PROVINCIAL BORDERS AND WERE BANNED BY THE CHINESE GOVERNMENT

	Cult/sect	Chinese name	Founder/key leader	Origin	Year founded/ spread	Year banned
1	Shouters[1]	Huhan pai	Witness Lee (Li Changshou)	U.S.A.	1960s–1970s	1983
2	Shouters 2[1]	Changshouzhu jiao	He Enjie/Zhao Weishan	China	1980s	1995
3	Established King[1]	Beili wang	Wu Yangming	Anhui	1988	1992
4	Lightning from the East (All Mighty God; Actual God)[1]	Dongfang shandian/ Quanneng Shen/Shiji Shen	Deng (?)/ Zhao Weishan	Henan	1991	1995
5	Lord God Sect[1]	Zhushen jiao	Liu Jiaguo	Hunan	1993	1995
6	Lingling Sect	Lingling jiao	Hua Xuehe	Jiangsu	1983	1991
7	All Scope Church[2]	Quanfanwei jiaohui	Xu Yongze	Henan	1984	1988
8	South China Church[2]	Huanan jiaohui	Gong Shengliang	Hubei	1990	2001

(continued)

Table 5.2

(continued)

	Cult/sect	Chinese name	Founder/key leader	Origin	Year founded/ spread	Year banned
9	Disciples Sect (Narrow Gate)	Mentu hui (kuangye zhaimen)	Ji Sanbao	Shaanxi	1989	1990
10	Three Ranks of Servants	Sanban puren	Xu Shengguang; Huo Congguang	Henan	1980s	1999
11	Cold Water Sect	Lengshui jiao	Wu Huanxing (?)	Guangdong	1985/1988	1991/1999
12	Commune Sect	Fanwugongyong pai	Liang Jiaye	Shandong	1991	1994
13	New Testament Church/Apostles Faith Sect	Xinyue Jiaohui/ Shitu xinxin hui	Zhang Lude/ Zuo Kun	Taiwan	1964/1988	1995
14	Resurrection Sect	Fuhuo Dao	Guo Guangxu; Wen Qiuhui	Henan	1996	1999

15	Dami Evangelism Association	*Dami Xuanjiaohui*	Li Changlin	South Korea	1988/1992	1995
16	World Elijah Evangelism Association	*Shijie Yiliya Fuyin Xuanjiaohui*	Piao Minghu	South Korea	1980/1993	1996

Note: 1. These five cults were closely related; later ones were split-off cults.
2. These two groups were related, and the latter split off from the former. There are disagreements among overseas Christians regarding their Christian orthodoxy.

Sources: Shixiong Li and Xiqiu Fu, eds., *China's Religious Freedom and "State Secrets" (PRC Classified Documents)* (New York: Committee for Investigation on Persecution of Religion in China, 2002); Center for Religious Freedom, *Report Analyzing Seven Secret Chinese Government Documents*; Susanna Chen, ed., *Discerning Truth from Heresies: A Critical Analysis of the Alleged and Real Heresies in Mainland China* (Taipei: Christianity and China Research Center 2000); Emily Clare Dunn, *Heterodoxy and Contemporary Chinese Protestantism: The Case of Eastern Lightning*, PhD dissertation, University of Melbourne, 2010.

The Chinese government has also banned non-Christian groups that originated in other countries, such as the Unification Church, the Baha'i, Mormonism, the Children of God, the True Buddha Sect, the Kuanyin Dharma Gate, and so on. Nonetheless, these groups have continued to be present in China. Many of the traditional cultic groups (*hui-dao-men*) that originated from traditional folk religion have also been revived.[25] Among these, the most notorious is Yiguan Dao, which was the largest group before 1949 and was severely suppressed by the Communist government in the 1950s. Today, it has been brought back by businesspeople from Taiwan, where it survived the Kuomingtang government's suppression and became legal in the 1980s. Underground Buddhists, Daoists, and Muslims also exist. Among the ethnic separatists are some of the Tibetan Buddhists and Uyghur Muslims.[26] The authorities have carried out repeated and severe crackdowns on these separatists.

The costs of engaging in the black market of religion in China are very high. Once found by the authorities, leaders and active believers may suffer psychological abuse, physical torture, monetary fines, temporary detention, labor camps, prison terms, and even death penalties. For example, Reverend Gong Shengliang, the founder of the South China Church, was sentenced to death by a court in Hubei Province in 2001. Following the outcry of human-rights groups such as Amnesty International, the Freedom House's Center for Religious Freedom, and many Christian groups and under political pressure from Western governments, the sentence was changed to life imprisonment. Many lesser-known religious leaders have been sentenced and executed without international notice. In spite of these dangers, black-market religion cannot be wiped out. Sectarian groups such as the

Shouters have been banned since the early 1980s, but more than twenty years later, they are still active in many parts of China. After some leaders were rounded up, new leadership and groups sprang up with even more radical beliefs and practices. Moreover, novel groups keep emerging.

On the other hand, although the high costs of engaging in black-market activities have not deterred religious virtuosos, the high costs are unbearable to a majority of people. When religious needs cannot be met in the open market and the potential costs are too great in the black market, many people seek alternatives in the gray market.

THE GRAY MARKET

The gray market of religion is very complex. The boundaries between the gray market, the open market, and the black market are vague, elastic, and constantly shifting. In any society, informal religious and spiritual activities are difficult to document, and the political restrictions in China present additional obstacles to data collection. At the present, only some broad brush strokes may be offered to illustrate the gray market's huge size and complexity. Here I offer a description of the gray market in terms of two general categories: (1) explicitly religious phenomena and (2) implicitly religious phenomena. Explicitly religious phenomena include illegal activities of legal religious organizations and individuals and ambiguous groups and activities sponsored by government agencies or officials. Implicitly religious phenomena include religions expressed as culture and as health science.

The first type of gray-market religion is explicitly religious. It is worth noting that government-sanctioned religious groups and individuals have undertaken illegal religious activities. The authorities have imposed various restrictions on the five religions supervised by the "patriotic" associations. For instance, no proselytizing is allowed outside the approved religious premises. However, most religions are proselytizing religions, and the urge to proselytize is difficult to suppress. In fieldwork visits to aboveground churches in large coastal cities and small inland cities, I met or heard about pastors who had ventured out to preach at unapproved "gathering points" (*juhui dian*). They did it discreetly, of course, but also with practical justification. They commonly asserted that had they not done so, those gathering points might have been in greater danger of influence by heretical sects or evil cults, which would disturb social stability, a paramount concern of the current regime. Indeed, the house churches have spread quickly in both rural and urban China. They are not approved by or registered with the government, and in some cases, their applications for registration were denied or withheld without a decision. Their religious worship services are not really underground. They operate in the gray area of the regulations.

In cities such as Shanghai and Beijing, scholars have observed numerous so-called private Buddhist temples, chapels within private homes or in office buildings. Their operation is similar to that of the Protestant house churches. Many Daoist ritual specialists (*huo ju dao shi*) are active in the provinces along the Yangtze River.[27] They are comparable to the so-called Protestant self-claimed evangelists (*zi feng chuan dao ren*), who are subject to crackdowns. I have also learned of the existence of Buddhist monks or Tibetan lamas leading meditation and sutra study sessions at believers' homes or in office suites rented for such activities. Some of the local officials of the RAB seem to be aware of such activities, but many watch them with "one eye closed" unless the activities became too conspicuous. For example, the government-sanctioned Nanjing Theological Seminary has had faculty members and students discreetly preaching at unregistered house churches. In 1999, three such students were ordered to quit school; in 2000, a faculty member, Ji Tai, was dismissed from the seminary.

Similarly, clergy members in the Catholic Patriotic Association also engage in activities that the government considers illegal. Although the authorities forbid Catholics to have organizational connections with the Vatican, it has been reported that more than two-thirds of the bishops in the government-sanctioned church have quietly received "apostolic mandates," or official approval, from the Vatican. Consequently, "There is now no clear distinction between an open church which the government controls politically and an underground church which it does not."[28] The authorities have failed to stop part of the red market from turning gray. On the other hand, the Vatican issued a letter from Pope Benedict XVI to the Catholics in China in 2007, calling for reconciliation between underground and aboveground communities. This has made the Catholics in the red and black markets further blended into the gray market.

Another manifestation of the explicitly religious type in the gray market is, ironically, sponsored by certain government agencies or individual officials, who do so mostly for political or economic reasons. For example, in order to bring Taiwan closer to mainland China through direct links of transportation and commerce, a goal adamantly resisted by Taiwanese authorities for several years, Chinese authorities have restored and rebuilt Mazu temples in Meizhou, Fujian, the legendary birthplace of the girl who eventually came to be worshipped as the goddess Mazu or Tianhou. The intent was to encourage Mazu worshippers in Taiwan to take homage trips, which would pose pressures on the Taiwanese government to open direct links with the mainland. For similarly political considerations, the authorities have allowed traditional religions to be revived among ethnic minority groups, such as the Dongba religion among the Naxi people in Yunnan, the Buluotuo or Mo religion among the Zhuang people in Guangxi Zhuang Autonomous Region, and the Nuo religion among the Tujia people in Guizhou and Hubei.[29]

A major reason for government agencies to support temple revivals is that they wish to attract overseas Chinese investments and businesses. "Build the religious stage to sing the economic opera" (*zongjiao datai, jingji changxi*) is the primary intent, and many local governments have put this strategy into practice, essentially pouring oil on the fire of religious revivals. Falling into this category are some Huang Daxian (Wong Tai Sin in Cantonese) temples. In 1984, when Lang and Ragvald started their study of the Huang Daxian temple in Hong Kong, no Huang Daxian temple existed in mainland China, because all of them had been destroyed. By 2001, however, at least a dozen Huang Daxian temples had been rebuilt in Guangdong and Zhejiang Provinces. Moreover, six of the ten temples documented in the study "were founded with the support and sometimes at the initiative of agencies of the local government."[30] In fact, in 2005, the Zhejiang Province organized in the city of Jianhua a "Huangdaxian Cultural Tourism Festival," and several provincial officials and the director of the State Administration of Religious Affairs, Ye Xiaowen, officiated at the opening ceremony.

The agencies involved in temple-reviving projects include the Tourist Bureau, the Cultural Affairs Bureau, and the

Preservation of Historic Sites Bureau of a local government. By 1996, the construction of temples and outdoor Buddha statues had become so widespread that the central government issued a circular to curb the craze. Consequently, many temples were torn down, some were converted to secular uses, and others were co-opted into the existing Daoist or Buddhist "patriotic" associations. This shows the ambivalence of the authorities who, on the one hand, hope to promote economic development and, on the other hand, uphold the atheist ideology. It also reflects the complex orientations and priorities of the various bureaus at the different levels of government.

When explicitly religious organizations and activities are restricted and curbed, many individuals resort to more implicit forms of religion. When they carry out activities in the name of culture or science, no religious regulation applies, even if most scholars in the West normally classify such groups and activities as religious. According to C. K. Yang, in traditional Chinese society, alongside the institutional religions there existed a so-called diffused religion,[31] which I would further differentiate into semireligious and quasi-religious elements that are intimately merged in the secular institutions and social life, as discussed in chapter 2 above. Between 1949 and 1979, the authorities tried hard to extract and expel such religious elements from the secular institutions. Since 1979, however, such semi- and quasi-religious beliefs and practices have come back. However, up to now, such elements mostly have returned in the name of culture, not religion per se, for "culture" is a neutral or positive concept without ideological weight, as discussed in chapter 3 above.

The government has restored many temples in order to reap the economic benefits of tourism. It has also restored temples dedicated to the ancient and legendary kings of Yan,

Huang, Yao, Shun, and Yu, with the intention of strengthening cultural ties with all Chinese persons throughout the
world. Many villages and towns have revived popular practices, including building temples dedicated to historic heroes
and immortals who have become tutelage gods. They hold
dedication ceremonies, temple fairs, and festival celebrations.
These temples and activities are difficult to classify as either
Daoist or Buddhist, although they often include Daoist gods
and Buddhas or Bodhisattvas in their pantheons. Some may
be more organized than others, such as the Three-in-One
sect (*sanyi jiao*) in Fujian,[32] but most remain informal. The
whole village often supports the construction of such temples, and retired officials frequently organize the projects.
Most villagers and clansmen participate in the celebration of
festivals and fairs related to the temple. As such, these activities are regarded as part of the local cultural tradition or
folklore, rather than as part of religion itself. Revived local
communal religions and individual spiritualities have been
observed throughout the country.[33] In 2004 and 2005, several
state ministries and, finally, the State Council issued circulars
calling for protecting the "nonmaterial cultural heritage"
(*feiwuzhi wenhua yichan*); it has been under this name that
many folk-religious practices have been revived in the first
decade of the twenty-first century.

In addition, many households maintain an ancestral
altar or a shrine dedicated to gods and goddesses. Many clan
ancestral temples (*ci tang*) have also been rebuilt. I have also
seen many restaurants and businesses in Beijing, Guangzhou,
and other cities that conspicuously display an altar for the
Tudi (earth god) or Caishen (wealth god).

A more widespread manifestation of implicit religion
was *qigong* in the name of health science. The word *qigong*

means, literally, the power or exercise of *qi* (air or breathing). Simply put, *qigong* is a form of physical exercise, meditation, and healing. Not all *qigong* groups or practices are religious, as some of which are essentially similar to acrobatic exercises. But the *qigong* phenomenon in the PRC has been extremely complex, entangled with traditional Chinese medicine, modern scientism, body politics, and now international relations.[34] A detailed examination of *qigong* is beyond the scope of this chapter, but suffice it to say that most *qigong* groups and practices are a form of implicit religion. First, almost all large *qigong* groups offer an explanatory system that uses Buddhist and/or Daoist concepts and theories. Only a very few rudimentary *qigong* practices resemble the martial arts (*wu shu*) or general acrobatic exercises (*ti cao*) in claiming no supernatural elements. Second, most *qigong* masters claim to be heirs of certain ancient Daoist or Buddhist lineages and assert that they have been sent by the mystical masters to "go out of the mountains" (*chu shan*) and spread the *gong*. Third, the practices often involve meditating over religious images or cosmic principles, reciting mantras, and/or reading scriptures, broadly understood. For political and cultural reasons, *qigong* masters and practitioners have insisted that they were not religious, in order to avoid religious regulations. However, to some extent, they are comparable to New Age religions, occult beliefs and practices, magic, yoga, or "client and audience cults" in the West.[35] Some are well-organized new religious movements (NRMs).

Between 1979 and 1999, there were tens of thousands of *qigong* teachers and masters and thousands of *qigong* groups with many followers. Some large *qigong* groups established "cultivation and education bases" (*xiulian peixun jidi*) and "research centers" (*yanjiu zhongxin*) with magnificent buildings and organized hundreds or thousands of "cultivation points" (*liangong dian*), most of which were in public parks or streets. The largest and most effective ones became powerful economic enterprises and efficient organizations with enthusiastic cadres (see table 5.3).

Qigong groups also commonly adopted the latest scientific terms, insisting that they were related to science instead of religion. In fact, it was some top-ranked scientists holding high-level political positions who helped *qigong* take off with a bang in the 1980s. The most enthusiastic supporters of *qigong* included Qian Xuesen (Tsien Hsue-shen), father of China's aerospace science, and General Zhang Zhenhuan, head of the National Defense Science and Engineering Commission. Zhang later headed the China Qigong Scientific Research Council (*qigong kexue yanjiu hui*), which provided institutional legitimacy for many *qigong* groups. When a new *qigong* master emerged, if he managed to take a photo with Qian, Zhang, or some other top officials, he would instantly become a great master and soon attract hundreds and thousands of followers. Such photos with political figures not only served publicity purposes but also provided legitimization and protection to the leaders and followers.

Before 1999, most *qigong* groups existed in some sort of legitimate form, such as being affiliated with either the Physical Education and Sports Bureau or the Science and Technology Association (*keji xiehui*), both government agencies. Some of the less religiously oriented *qigong* masters were housed in hospitals as specialty physicians. However, the ambiguous nature of *qigong* groups had caused dissension within the party ranks from the very beginning. Since 1981, top party ideologues such as Yu Guangyuan have continually voiced strong

Table 5.3

A PARTIAL LIST OF WIDESPREAD MAJOR QIGONG GROUPS BY 1999

	Name	Chinese name	Founder	Origin	Founding year	Year banned
1	Guolin New Qigong	Guolin Xinqigong	Guo Lin	Beijing	1979	1999
2	Flying Crane Gong	Hexiangzhuang	Zhao xx, Pang Ming	Beijing	1980	1999
3	China Wisdom Power Gong	Huaxia Zhineng Gong	Pang Ming	Hebei	1985	1999
4	Qian Dragon-gate Gong	Qianzi Longmen Gong	Su Xueliang	Beijing	1980s	1999
5	Yanxin Qigong	Yanxin Qigong	Yan Xin	Sichuan	1985	1999
6	Daoist Dragon-gate Sect	Daojia Longmen Pai	Wang Liping	Beijing	1985?	1999
7	Greater Nature Center Gong	Daziran Zhongxin Gong	Zhang Xiangyu	Qinghai	1985	1990
8	Wisdom Lotus Gong	Huilian Gong	Chen Linfeng	Beijing	1986	1999
9	Zhong Gong	Zhong Gong	Zhang Hongbao	Beijing	1987	1999
10	Huitong Dantian Gong	Huitong Dantian Gong	Zhang Yulei	Baoding, Hebei	1987	1999

(continued)

Table 5.3

(continued)

	Name	Chinese name	Founder	Origin	Founding year	Year banned
11	Jingjin Neidan Gong	Jingjin Neidan Gong	Wang Qinyu	Chengdu, Sichuan	1987?	1999
12	Fragrance Gong	Xiang Gong	Tian Ruisheng	Luoyang, Henan	1988	1999
13	Zhonghua Shengong	Zhonghua Shengong	Zhu Zhenggao	Qingdao, Shandong	1988	1999
14	All Dimensions Return to One	Wanfa Guiyi	Zhang Xiaoping (*fozi*)	Huhhot, Neimong	1989	1995
15	Bodhi Gong	Puti Gong	Di Yuming	Guangdong, Guangdong	1991	1999
16	Shenchang Bodily Science	Shenchang Renti Keji	Shen Chang	Suzhou, Jiangsu	1991	1999
17	Falun Gong	Falun Gong	Li Hongzhi	Jilin	1992	1999

criticisms of the so-called paranormal power (*teyi gongneng*) and called for restriction.[36] As a result, around 1990, a few overly religious *qigong* masters were prosecuted and jailed.

Among the largest *qigong* groups, Falun Gong came in late. Soon after its launching in 1992, however, it swept the country. Its fast spread was partly a result of its religious nature and its increasingly religious overtones in a receptive culture.[37] Initially, it registered with the China Qigong Scientific Research Council. However, its religious overtones quickly caused concerns, and Falun Gong was subsequently deregistered in 1996. Some Falun Gong leaders then sought to affiliate with the China Buddhist Association but failed. At this time, Falun Gong had already gained millions of followers all over China and had spread globally to the United States, Australia, and other countries. In 1999, Falun Gong made a bold move by gathering more than 10,000 followers to surround Zhongnanhai, the headquarters of the CCP and the central government, to demand official legalization of Falun Gong. The authorities responded with a determined crackdown and banned it as an "evil cult" (*xie jiao*). Following this, Zhong Gong, Xiang Gong, and other large *qigong* groups were all tagged as evil cults and were banned; their key leaders were prosecuted, properties confiscated, and practices prohibited. In fact, all *qigong* groups were disbanded or deregistered. Finally, the China Qigong Scientific Research Council was officially deregistered by the State Civil Affairs Department in the summer of 2003. The group practice of *qigong* in the park in the morning, a ubiquitous scene all over China in the 1980s and 1990s, has essentially disappeared since 1999.

Making *qigong* illegal has blackened a significant part of the gray market. However, with millions of followers in each of the major *qigong* groups, the ban has not been able to halt *qigong* practices completely. Suppressed in the public sphere, some *qigong* practitioners went underground, just as some Christians did in the 1950s. Falun Gong followers have persisted despite severe crackdowns. On the other hand, the number of practitioners seems small. Most of the former *qigong* practitioners have stopped practicing. In many conversations with relatives, friends, and acquaintances who once practiced *qigong*, I find that most of them have given up practicing *qigong*, and some of them have converted to Buddhism or Christianity.

After a pause of several years, some *qigong* groups have managed to reemerge, albeit under new names and with great caution. For example, Guolin New Qigong followers now practice in public parks under the name Guolin Fitness Way (*guolin jianshen fa*). The religious or supernatural words are removed or significantly toned down, at least in public. Several major *qigong* groups have been quietly regrouping through Internet Web sites, exploring ways to go public again. In 2004, the *jianshen qigong* (health-oriented *qigong*), which is stripped of any reference to the supernatural, regained legal status under the supervision of the China Physical Education and Sports Bureau. However, a major challenge for the regulators is determining how to distinguish and certify health *qigong* masters from the sectarian ones.

How large is the gray market of religion in China today? Based on various estimates, one may say that there are about 100 million people engaged in the red market and between 100 million and 200 million people engaged in the black market. If these estimates are close to reality, it means that about 1 billion people are neither in the open market nor in the black market of religion. Are these 1 billion Chinese really irreligious, or are they simply engaged in the gray market of religion? In 2007, the Horizon Consultancy Group, a well-established survey company in China, conducted the "Chinese Spiritual Life Survey." The nationwide representative sample, excluding Tibet and Xinjiang Autonomous Regions because of impracticability, includes 7,021 cases. My preliminary analysis of the data shows that 85 percent of the respondents either held some religious beliefs or had some religious practices in the last twelve months, even though most of them did not identify with a religion.[38]

A survey of young people in Shanghai also provides some indication. The survey was conducted in 1995 by the Shanghai Chinese Communist Youth League (CCYL).[39] The respondents were young people within the reach of the CCYL. If there is any bias in the sample, it is probably overrepresentative of more "progressive" young people who were closer to the CCP's atheist ideology. Surprisingly, however, only 18 percent of the respondents clearly rejected the so-called superstitious beliefs (*mixin*)—*suan gua* (fortune telling), *ce zi* (glyphomancy, analyzing the parts of Chinese characters), *xiang mian* (physiognomy, face reading); 42 percent said that they "do not completely believe but cannot disbelieve"; 31 percent were "curious about it but do not believe"; and 8 percent said "it is hard to say." Perhaps more surprising is that the proportion of clear rejection is not really different from that in the U.S. population. For example, the 1994 General Social Survey included a question on astrology, and only 19 percent of Americans said that it was definitely not true, and the rest chose answers from among "probably not true," "can't say," "probably true," or "definitely true."

Note that some religious believers in the open and black markets, such as conservative Protestants and certain

Buddhists, would also reject these paranormal beliefs. Without better measurements for comparison, these findings are at least indicative that Chinese openness toward supernatural beliefs is probably not much lower than that of Americans. The difference between the Chinese and the Americans is not that the Chinese are naturally irreligious and the Americans are innately religious, but that the U.S. religious market is exceedingly mobilized, whereas the Chinese religious market is seriously underdeveloped.

If 85 percent of the Chinese population is at least open toward supernatural beliefs or participating in religious practices, but only small minorities have been recruited into either the government-approved religions or the underground ones, there exists a huge gray market with hundreds of millions of potential religious consumers. Perhaps many of these individuals have unmet religious needs, or their religious consciousness is waiting to be awakened. Many may consciously or unconsciously engage in the gray market of implicitly religious groups or spiritual entrepreneurs. Such a huge gray market is destined to be a fertile ground for new religious movements. Further discussion of religious awakening continues in the next chapter.

DYNAMICS OF THE TRIPLE MARKETS

The triple-market model provides a broad framework to sort various kinds of religious phenomena into a conceptual order. The gray-market concept is central in this model; it accentuates the noninstitutionalized religiosity that has been largely neglected in studies of religion, especially the economic approach, that focus on American and European societies. The gray market includes all religious and spiritual organizations, practitioners, and activities that have an ambiguous legal status. Some of the groups and practices are so ambiguous that scholars of religious studies may find it difficult or controversial to classify them as religious. Nonetheless, such spiritual alternatives compete with conventional religions in the religious marketplace.

The analysis in this chapter illustrates that the boundaries of the tripartite market are not clear-cut but are constantly shifting. During the eradication period from 1966 to 1979, no open market existed. All religious organizations and activities were repressed so severely that religion could exist only in the black market or the gray market in the form of the Mao personality cult. Since 1979, some religious groups have been legalized. However, deciding which religious groups are to be allowed or banned is a constant challenge for regulators and regulation enforcers. CCP agencies, the central government, and provincial and local governments are not always on the same page in regard to particular religious groups and activities. For example, some local governments have encouraged, and even sponsored, restoring temples for the purpose of attracting overseas investment, but the central government curbed this frenzy by ordering most of the new buildings torn down. However, some of the temples built this way were co-opted into "patriotic" religious associations and were therefore moved from the gray market into the red market. Adam Chau's study of a popular religious temple provides a good example of a gray-market religion turned to the red market.[40] The Temple of the Black Dragon King in northern Shaanxi was eventually co-opted into the Daoist Association. Throughout the 1980s and

1990s, *qigong* groups were allowed or even encouraged by various government officials and legalized by certain government agencies other than the Religious Affairs Bureau. Since 1999, however, all sectarian *qigong* groups have been disbanded, thus turning these gray-market groups black.

When stronger regulations blacken previously gray-market segments, two consequences are inevitable: (1) the black market is enlarged, and (2) the gray market is emptied. Criminalization will likely reduce the total number of religious adherents of those groups, because not all people want to practice in the underground, but the emptied gray market opens up space for new and innovative suppliers. The level of volatility in the gray market increases as entrepreneurial individuals and groups rise to fill the emptied niches. The ambiguity of gray-market practices makes it difficult to regulate or enforce regulations.

To what extent can the state efficiently control religion through regulation? Obviously, the efficacy of state power has been exaggerated in regard to both Western societies (claiming that deregulation would lead to the demise of religion)[41] and China (believing that state suppression would eradicate religion).[42] The triple-market theory shows that market forces are at work, and religious groups and believers may not respond in ways that the regulators want. Heavy regulation cannot effectively reduce religion. It can only complicate the religious market by pushing religious organizations and believers into the black and gray markets. Under heavy regulation, the gray market is not only huge but also volatile, providing a fertile ground for new religious movements. For regulators and regulation enforcers, the gray market means an unmanageable state of religious affairs.

THE SHORTAGE ECONOMY OF

RELIGION UNDER COMMUNISM

WHEN A GOVERNMENT imposes its ideology and sup-
presses its competitors, to what extent can it succeed?
Throughout human history, many regimes have sought to
establish a state religion and eradicate all competitors. In
the recent past, the Soviet-bloc governments tried to
impose the Communist ideology on the people and suppress all religions. China went even further, experimenting
with a ban on all religions for more than a decade. Despite
the best efforts of the Party-state, religion survived. The
Chinese government has also failed to keep religion at a
reduced level during the reform era since 1979. All kinds of
religions are thriving in China today. The restrictive regulations that intend to keep religion at a low level have
instead created vivacious dynamics on the demand side,
which, I argue, is characteristic of a shortage economy of
religion. While the triple-market model describes the complex tripartite economy of religion, this chapter articulates
a shortage-economy theory that underpins the triple-
market complexity.

DEMAND-DYNAMICS MODEL IN A RELIGIOUS SHORTAGE ECONOMY

In a shortage economy, according to János Kornai,[1] the shortage of supply shapes consumer behaviors in crucial ways: "Those living in a shortage economy experience day by day that the buyer is at the mercy of the seller."[2] Kornai developed an economics of shortage to explain the economy of the socialist system under Communist rule. People who lived in prereform China or other socialist countries can attest that buying goods was a process full of frustration and ordeal. Popular humor held that the most frequently used expression by salesclerks was "*meiyou*" ("don't have it") and that people frequently rushed to get into a long waiting line before knowing what was available at the front of the line. Besides their experiences of frustration, individuals adapt in different ways. "Shortages cause loss and inconvenience to consumers. They often have to wait for supply, to queue up, and frequently, are forced to be content with goods different from their original wish."[3] This brief statement by Kornai may serve as a good starting point for a more systematic analysis of the demand-side dynamics in the religious economy.

Following Kornai, let us take, for example, a woman preparing to buy beef. "Unless lucky, her shopping is not a single action but a process, a sequence of decisions" with multiple stages of action.[4] When the desired good—beef—is available, the consumer's behavior is self-evident, *buying* it, or *queuing up* to buy it in case there are many buyers on the spot. If the desired good is not available in sight, she may embark on a trip, or trips, to search for it. *Searching* would end if she later finds the intended good. But she may also choose one of the other two alternatives to searching: *substituting*, such as buying pork instead of beef, or simply giving up the intent to buy, that is, *suppressing* the desire for eating beef. If the desired good is a kind of staple food, however, as time goes by, substituting and suppressing may not be retainable. She may revert to searching and buying if the previously desired good becomes available again. Applying these concepts of consumer behaviors in a shortage economy to the religious economy under Communist rule, we expect to see people *queuing up, searching, suppressing demand,* and *experimenting with substitutes* for religion (see figure 6.1).

Kornai stops short of elaborating further upon consumer behaviors at the macro level. Instead, he turns his primary attention to the producers, especially to the "soft-budget constraints" on the producers in a shortage economy. Examining the supply side in a shortage economy of religion is certainly important to do. However, in an economy where demand chronically exceeds supply, the demand-side change

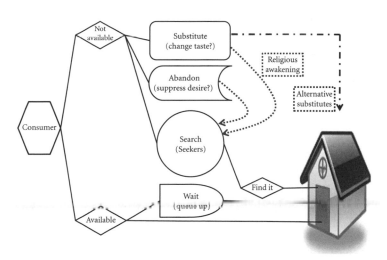

FIGURE 6.1 Demand-Side Dynamics in a Shortage Economy of Religion.

is the primary driver in the interactions between demand and supply under regulation. Thus, this chapter focuses on the demand-side dynamics in the religious shortage economy in China.

Demand-side dynamics is the overarching characteristic of the religious shortage economy. Historically, the persistent demand for religion was that which forced the Communists to abandon the ideology-driven eradication measures, as described in chapter 4 above. Further, once religion was granted limited tolerance in the reform era, the demand for religion has been continuously increasing and surpassing the regulated supply. In this process, the continual "excessive demand" for religion seems to have caught the central planners and regulators off-guard. After all, there was no theory to predict this, for neither the ideological orthodoxy of Marxism-Leninism-Maoism nor the other secularization theories with which the Chinese Communist theoreticians became familiar would account for this unexpected growth in demand for religion within a modernizing society. Even the economic approach by Rodney Stark and his associates, which has been rightfully labeled as "supply-side explanations" by themselves, has very much ignored the demand side in theorizing, oversimplistically assuming the stability of demand.

The Party-state tried hard to eliminate religion from society, but such efforts failed, and religion survived. Religious regulations have remained strict in reform-era China. However, the strict regulations have not achieved their goals of containing religion at a low level in society. Instead, as chapter 5 describes, it has resulted in the triple markets, in which many religious activities operate in the underground or in legally ambiguous areas. Let us now review what has happened to the demand side in response to the regulations.

ERADICATION FAILED

The ban on religion took effect in 1966 during the zenith of the Cultural Revolution, when all religious sites were closed down, many temples and churches torn apart, religious scriptures burned, statues of gods and religious artifacts smashed, and believers forced to make public renunciations or be sent to prisons or *laogai* (reeducation through labor) camps.

Ironically, the eradication measures created martyrs or living heroes who inspired other believers. Among the tens of thousands of intractable believers, the most well known are the Catholic and Protestant leaders: the Catholic bishop Gong Pinmei (Kung Pingmei, 1901–2000) in Shanghai, who was jailed between 1955 and 1985 before being exiled to the United States; Protestant minister Wang Mingdao (1900–1991) in Beijing, who was jailed between 1955 and 1979; Watchman Nee (1903–1972), the founder of the Little Flock Christian sect, who was jailed in 1952 and died in prison in 1972; Yuan Xiangchen (1914–2005) in Beijing, who was jailed between 1957 and 1979; Lin Xian'gao (Samuel Lamb, 1924–) in Guangzhou, who was jailed between 1955 and 1978. Some staunch believers, such as Lamb and Yuan, survived in and out of prisons and labor camps and have become the most renowned Protestant house-church leaders in the 1980s and 1990s.[5]

During the religious ban, some Christian groups managed to hold religious gatherings in secrecy at home or in the wilderness.[6] As mentioned in chapter 5, in the coastal city of Wenzhou, some Christians never stopped gathering to worship during the Cultural Revolution; they continued to hold worship services at night in the mountains. Christians in many other regions similarly practiced in secrecy. A monk of the Buddhist

Shaolin Temple in Henan Province told people that more than a dozen monks refused to return to their original villages during the Cultural Revolution. They stayed at the temple and became farmers in the "People's Commune" (*renmin gongshe*) but secretly kept practicing meditation and sutra recitation. I have also heard and read many stories of imprisoned Christians holding fast to their faith while in prison for many years. Evidently, eradication measures, despite their intensity, failed to eliminate religious believers and practitioners.

As it became apparent that religion could not be wiped out of people's minds and hearts in the near future, the more pragmatic Deng Xiaoping led the Chinese CCP in a change of course. To rally the nation for economic reform and development, CCP authorities conceded to the religious demand, albeit with firm reservations. Beginning in 1979, a limited number of temples, mosques, and churches were reopened for religious activities. In 1982, the CCP issued Document No. 19, "The Basic Viewpoint and Policy on the Religious Affairs during the Socialist Period of Our Country," which restated the limited tolerance to five religions and set the basis for the current religious policy. Nevertheless, Document No. 19 offered consolation for having reduced the proportion of religious believers within the population. In essence, then, the shift of position is merely from militant atheism to enlightenment atheism, while the religious policy is still firmly based on atheism.

DEMAND SUPPRESSED

Indeed, eradication failed only in the sense that persevering believers have survived the harshest eradication campaigns.

However, although religious demand was never reduced to zero, the active demand for religion in China was effectively reduced to a minuscule level.

Religious demand is difficult to measure, as some individuals may secretly hold religious beliefs and say silent prayers without public expression or participation in religious activities. To stay within the empirical limit of what is observable, we may use a proxy of religious demand: the expressed interest in and practice of religion, which may be considered active demand. In comparison with other societies, in China, the proportion of people who admit to having religious beliefs and practices remains extremely low. According to the World Values Surveys,[7] the overall level of religiosity in the People's Republic of China is the lowest among all of the countries included in the surveys (see table 6.1). In the 2000 wave of the survey that included China for the first time, only 13.7 percent of the Chinese in the sample (N = 1,000) claimed to be religious, and only 6.0 percent belonged to a religion, the lowest percentage among the sixty-seven countries in the survey. For the sixty-seven countries, the averages reported were 77.7 percent and 67.0 percent, respectively. Meanwhile, 88.9 percent of the Chinese reported that they never or practically never attended religious services, whereas the average was 22.7 percent; and 24.0 percent of the Chinese claimed to be convinced atheists, while the average was 4.2 percent.

Some people might suggest that the Chinese have always been a nonreligious people, but such a speculative claim is contrary to empirical observations. For decades, the received wisdom has been that the Chinese populous as a whole has never been religious. Hu Shih, one of the most influential Chinese intellectuals in the twentieth century, asserts, "China is a country without religion and the Chinese are a people

Table 6.1

RELIGIOUSNESS IN THE PEOPLE'S REPUBLIC OF CHINA, TAIWAN, AND OTHER COUNTRIES

	P.R. China (N=1,000) %	Average of All 67 Countries %	Taiwan (N=780) %
INDEPENDENT OF WHETHER YOU ATTEND CHURCH/TEMPLE OR NOT, WOULD YOU SAY YOU ARE A RELIGIOUS PERSON?			
A religious person	13.7	67.0	72.2
Not a religious person	55.3	19.9	22.1
A convinced atheist	24.0	4.2	1.7
No answer	0.2	0.8	0.0
Don't know	6.8	4.0	4.1
DO YOU BELONG TO A RELIGIOUS DENOMINATION?			
No	93.0	18.9	20.9
Yes	6.0	77.7	79.1
No answer	0.0	0.2	0.0
Don't know	0.4	0.4	0.0
Not asked in survey	0.0	2.6	0.0
Missing	0.6	0.1	0.0

APART FROM WEDDINGS, FUNERALS AND CHRISTENINGS,
ABOUT HOW OFTEN DO YOU ATTEND RELIGIOUS SERVICES?

More than once a week	0.7	13.2	2.9
Once a week	1.5	18.5	4.0
Once a month	0.9	10.7	7.3
Only on special holy days	5.4	18.5	20.9
Once a year	0.8	6.3	2.3
Less often	1.0	8.3	22.4
Never or practically never	88.9	22.7	38.6
No answer	0.0	0.4	0.1
Don't know	0.8	0.3	1.4
Not asked in survey	0.0	1.2	0.0

Source: World Value Surveys, People's Republic of China and 66 other countries, 2000; Taiwan, 1995.

who are not bound by religious superstitions."[8] Many Chinese scholars and Western sinologists share this view.[9] However, this is a problem of armchair philosophers and theologians who read texts instead of observing people. Anthropologists and sociologists who have been there and done observations report a totally different reality: "There was not one corner in the vast land of China [before 1949] where one did not find temples, shrines, altars, and other places of worship [which] were a visible indication of the strong and pervasive influence of religion in Chinese society."[10]

Other people may question the validity of the World Values Surveys. An obvious concern would be language barriers or translation problems in such cross-national surveys. Were the questions accurately translated into Chinese? Furthermore, are the religious terms translatable at all without distorting or twisting the meaning? These could be real problems but would not support the speculative claim that the Chinese have always been less religious. In the 1995 wave of the surveys, the WVS included Taiwan, a Chinese society that shares much with mainland China in terms of language and culture. Answering the same set of questions, people in Taiwan reported a much higher religiosity, closer to the averages in the whole survey (see the right-hand column of Table 6.1). The huge difference between mainland China and Taiwan cannot be explained away merely by impugning methodological problems. The empirical findings of religiosity in Taiwan should also put the cultural-difference argument to rest. The differences are not cultural but political.

Of course, it is possible that some PRC respondents were not willing to admit their real views on religion, especially when religion is both politically suppressed and socially discouraged. If this is the case, it further indicates the importance of social and political factors in suppressing an *active demand* for religion.[11]

A recent survey of the Chinese spiritual life conducted by the Horizon Research Consultancy Group also seems to indicate a pattern of low religiosity in Chinese society.[12] Meanwhile, observers and researchers have noticed that a majority of Chinese immigrants and international students in the United States show indifference to religion, even though a substantial proportion, perhaps one-third, have converted to Christianity. No survey data are available yet to quantify this. However, the impression results from my many years of fieldwork research and is shared by some other scholars of Chinese immigrants and students in the United States.[13]

FORCED SUBSTITUTION

In place of religion, the CCP has tried to indoctrinate people with Communist beliefs, a common practice in Marxist-Leninist states:[14] "Within Marxist movements, and under Marxist-Leninist regimes, then, many devoted party activists and some average citizens accepted Marxian teachings *as if* they were a religious body of sacred precepts. Marxism, as a code of personal and group practices, satisfied emotional needs, provided transcendental guidance, and defined ethical ends."[15]

Some scholars have studied Communism as a sort of religion, such as a civil religion or a political religion.[16] However, labeling Communism as a religion is controversial at best.[17] As staunch atheists, the Communists themselves insist on the irreligious or antireligious nature of the Communist ideology. As such, it is more appropriate to call

Communism what it wants to be: a substitute for religion, or a pseudo-religion in the broad religious economy, as defined in chapter 2 above.

The CCP insistently propagates Communism as the "loftiest ideal and noblest belief" (*zui chonggao de lixiang he xinyang*). The Communist ideological system includes beliefs in an ideal future Communist Society, which is, in religious terms, like a paradise on earth, a society where no exploitation or inequality exists; the principle of production and distribution will be "from each according to his ability, to each according to his need," a common expression that could be found in standard textbooks in China. In order to advance into the Communist Society, revolutionary and progressive people need both to offer unrelenting service to the people and the Communist Party and to struggle against class enemies, that is, the counterrevolutionary and reactionary elements within society, including religious believers.

The organizational pillar upholding the Communist ideology lies in the organization of the Chinese Communist Party. In addition, the Chinese Communist Youth League (CCYL) for young individuals ages fourteen to twenty-eight, is a preparatory organization for the CCP. The CCP and the CCYL are selective, open only to people who, in principle, have demonstrated their commitment to the Communist endeavor. CCP and CCYL membership requires allegiance to Marxist dialectical materialism and historical materialism and open denunciation of any belief in gods, spirits, or ghosts. The Chinese Young Pioneers (*shao xian dui*, CYP), for elementary- and middle-school children ages six to fourteen, is organized "to prepare the Communist successors" (*jie ban ren*). Its membership criteria are less stringent, so that a majority of students may join. Nonetheless, to become a member, it is required to take a Communist vow: "I am determined to follow the teachings of the Chinese Communist Party, study hard, work hard, labor hard, and be prepared to sacrifice all for the Communist endeavor!"[18]

CCP and CCYL committees and branches are instituted in all grass-roots work units, residential districts, villages, schools, and universities, and the CYP is found in all elementary and middle schools. The grass-roots Party and League branches are responsible for organizing periodical study meetings for all members; the contents of the study are CCP and CCYL circulars, writings of the Communist leaders, or mutual criticism and self-criticism during a session about the organizational life (*zuzhi shenghuo*). Members are required to pay monthly membership dues to the Party or the League and to participate in organized activities (*guo zuzhi shenghuo*). There were 77,995,000 CCP members and 3,792,000 grass-roots committees and branches by the end of 2009,[19] 78,588,000 CCYL members and 2,836,000 grass-roots committees and branches by the end of 2008,[20] and about 130,000,000 CYP members in 350,000 brigades in 2010.[21] Together, CCP, CCYL, and CYP memberships of 286,583,000 represent about 21.5 percent of the total population,[22] which is more than any organized religion in China today.

Are the atheistic Communist campaigns effective? Many people have expressed their doubts, especially in light of the apparent disenchantment with Communist ideology during the reform era. However, in the World Values Surveys of 2000, one out of four Chinese respondents claimed to be "convinced atheists" (see Table 6.1), the highest proportion among all of the countries included in the survey. The level of effectiveness of the atheist propaganda may exceed many people's impressions and take some sobriety to sink in. In sociology, socialization is one of the fundamental concepts, which denotes that what is taught in the formative years of youth often, consciously or unconsciously, remains during the rest of life for most people. Some evidence appears to show that at least some Party and League members and aspirants appear to be genuinely inspired by Communist idealism. In a 1994 survey of young people in Shanghai conducted by the CCYL Shanghai Committee, nearly half of the respondents claimed that the purpose of joining the political organization, the CCP or CCYL, was "for pursuing the ideal and the belief" (*wei le lixiang he xinyang*), that is, the Communist ideal and belief.[23] Of course, the validity of this survey may be limited because it was conducted by the CCYL Shanghai Committee, and most of the respondents were "progressive young people" within its reach—83 percent of the respondents were either CCP members or CCYL members. The rest, one would suspect, more or less aspired to join CCP or CCYL. It is also difficult to know how many respondents gave politically correct answers under the circumstances. Nonetheless, based on my interviews and personal recollections with people in China, I tend to believe that at least some of the CCP and CCYL members are earnest believers in Communist idealism at least at some point.

For those CCP and CCYL members and aspirants who are more or less sincere, Communism is a substitute for religion. And it is a forced substitute for most of the people, because the alternatives were made inaccessible. According to János Kornai: "Forced substitution plays a major part in understanding the shortage syndrome. It should be distinguished from voluntary substitution. If a customer has hitherto chosen the first of two products, A and B, which are close substitutes for each other and both readily available on the supply side, and then changes to the other (substitutes B for A) because her tastes or the two products' relative prices have altered, the substitution can be considered voluntary. But if she buys B because A is unavailable, the substitution is forced."[24] In other words, "forced substitution" does not necessarily imply complete coercion. People always have choices, especially in the spiritual sphere. Communism is a forced substitute as religious alternatives are made unavailable or difficult to access.

Most Chinese people born in the PRC, especially those born before the 1980s, grew up without exposure to any religion. Not only were religious sites closed down, but textbooks and publications were also "sanitized" by atheism. From 1979 until recently, although some religious groups have been allowed to operate, there have been too few for most people to encounter in daily life. During my field research in a number of cities in China, I asked several times for directions to a nearby church or temple, but the local residents simply had no clue that there was a church or temple in the neighborhood, even though it was only about a hundred meters away from where we were standing. Moreover, even if some people came into contact with religious believers, the accepted atheist ideology, antireligious discourses, and lack of religious knowledge usually impeded their communication with believers and hindered their understanding of religious symbols, beliefs, and practices. Being fed by the standard textbook teaching of atheism, many people have habitually despised the religious clergy and looked down on religious believers. Even well-intentioned individuals often do not know how one correctly addresses a clergy person with respect and reverence, no matter what faith that clergy person belongs to.

ALTERNATIVE SUBSTITUTES

Not all of the substitutes are the same. Instead of the forced substitute, individuals may seek alternative substitutes. According to Kornai: "The customer abandons her original purchasing intention and instead buys something else that is more or less a substitute for it. It may be a close substitute, for instance, another kind of meat instead of beef, or a remoter substitute, some kind of deep frozen or canned meat, or it may be drawn from an even remoter sphere of substitutes: any kind of food stuff at all."[25]

Besides settling for the forced substitute offered in the official market, some consumers may also find unusual alternatives that are somewhat approximate to the desired good. For instance, when beef and other types of standard meat are not available at the shops, instead of settling for a vegetarian diet, the shopper mentioned earlier might choose to hunt herself for game animals or exotic insects for food. This kind of substitution may involve some unusual acts beyond the market scope, but life sometimes drives people to hunt and gather instead of shopping at the market. Many of my countrymen, especially my peers, did exactly that in the most difficult years during the Cultural Revolution, when the rationed food in my village was 165 kilograms per day per person, which is less than a third of a pound. Insects such as grasshoppers, cicadas, and gold beetles, along with frogs and pork fat, were considered precious delicacies. Even if these food types appear obnoxious to some people, such alternative substitutes were nonetheless more satisfactory and nutritious than total abstention from proteins.

A similar metaphor applies to the spiritual life. While some people have settled for Communism, other people have found that neither orthodox Communism nor irreligious materialism satisfies their spiritual needs. In such circumstances, they are suffering from an abstention from spiritual proteins. Therefore, many people have sought and experimented with spiritual alternatives that more closely approximate religion. Since these spiritual alternatives may be practiced without a religious label, form, or organization, they do not incur the same costs as practicing institutionalized religion under suppression.

During the Cultural Revolution, the major form of alternative spirituality was the personality cult of Chairman Mao, as described in chapters 4 and 5 above. The zest for Communism was surreptitiously replaced by the Mao personality cult. This may seem ironic, but it is not difficult to explain in the terms of economics of shortage. Noticeably, the personality cult is a common illness of Communist regimes: Mao in China, Stalin in the Soviet Union, Tito in Yugoslavia, Castro in Cuba, Ho Chi Minh in Vietnam, Kim Il-sung in North Korea. The forced substitute for religion—atheist Communism—gave way to an alternative substitute that deifies and worships the Communist leader. The individuals who practically worshipped Mao were experiencing feelings that were practically religious.

In reform-era China, two major forms of alternative spiritualities thrive without being labeled religious. One is conducted in the name of carrying on traditional culture (e.g., folk-religious practices). Another is carried out in the name of advancing science (e.g., healing cults of *qigong*). These make up the main elements in the gray market of religion, as described in chapter 5 above. Interestingly, the Communist leader Mao has been seen frequently among the tutelage gods of folk religion.[26]

Besides community-based folk religion, there are also popular beliefs and practices performed by individuals, including fortune telling (*suan gua*), physiognomy (*xiang mian*), glyphomancy (*ce zi*, analyzing the parts of written characters), fengshui, and the like. They have become widespread in the reform era. According to a report in *Religions in China*, the official magazine published by the State Religious Affairs Bureau, about 5 million individuals made a living through fortune telling in the mid-1990s.[27] Many cities have a de facto "fortune-telling street," with dozens of fortune tellers. Ironically, such a street is often in the vicinity of a university campus. A study by a researcher at the State Administration College has revealed that even a majority of Communist Party and government mid-level officials believe in some form of these superstitions.[28] Precisely speaking, these superstitions (*mixin*) are more magic than religious. Nonetheless, they include supernatural beliefs and meet people's needs for the supernatural to a certain extent.

When compared with the forced substitute of Communist ideology that rejects the supernatural, quasi-religious and even pseudo-religious practices can be found to be more satisfactory. However, the widespread practice of such noninstitutional spiritual beliefs is a symptom of the shortage economy of religion under heavy regulation, past or present. When institutional religions become more available or accessible, people who have practiced alternative spiritualities may find it less difficult than sincere atheists to turn to a conventional religion. Many testimonials of Buddhist converts that appeared in Buddhist magazines noted that practicing *qigong* had led these converts to becoming interested in Buddhism. For example, Venerable Master Jing Hui, the president of the Hebei Buddhist Association, said that in China, "many people begin to learn Chan [Buddhism] because they first practiced *qigong*."[29] Several people I have known for a long time have made a series of spiritual transitions, moving from professed Communist atheists to *qigong* practitioners to Falun Gong followers and then being baptized into the Christian church. Evidently, practicing folk religion, popular religion, or *qigong* has eased the way toward joining religion in more conventional forms. This is not to say that in a free market of religion, believers of folk religion will all join the institutionalized religion, as people's tastes and preferences vary widely yet are relatively stable among individuals. Just as eating bugs can become a habit, practicing an alternative spirituality can appear to be natural to some people, especially when it has been reinforced by various cultural and political forces within a society over a long time of history.

SPIRITUAL AWAKENING

Substituting may not last over time. Suppressing the active demand is not the same as wiping out the need, which could stay dormant or hidden in privacy. Once religion becomes available again, the dormant may be awakened, and the hidden need for religion may be revealed. This is illustrated in the dotted lines and boxes on the right side of figure 6.1.

The gradual spiritual awakening in reform-era China first appeared in the literature of creative writing. The 1981 novella "When the Sunset Clouds Disappear" (*Wanxia xiaoshi de shihou*) portrayed the protagonist, a Red Guard, as a man who had struggled with notions of science and Marxist dialectic materialism for many years. He ran into a Buddhist monk on the holy mountain of Taishan and engaged in a long, enlightening conversation. This novella instantly became politically controversial but popular among Chinese youth because of its departure from the ideological orthodoxy. It also stirred up heated debates among readers about science and religion. Religious clergy, once ridiculed and driven out of public sight, might hold some enlightening truths about the questions with which many young people were struggling. This idea itself was subversive at that time but stimulated truth seekers to begin their search in religion as well as in other realms.

Ten years later, the celebrated novelist Zhang Chengzhi, once a Red Guard himself, published the book *The History of a Soul* (*Xinling shi*), which features his embrace of his rediscovered Islamic identity. Gao Xingjian, the best-known Chinese writer in the West and winner of the 2000 Nobel Prize in Literature, has also written novels exploring spiritual themes with titles such as *The Soul Mountain* and *One Man's Bible* in the 1990s. His characters were obviously spiritual seekers, but they commonly ended up hopelessly wandering without finding a spiritual home. Indeed, many Chinese intellectuals have explored spiritual issues and sought religious answers, including novelists, poets, artists, and scholars.[30] Their publications have both reflected on and contributed to the growing popular interest in religion.

A case of the once suppressed need for religion reviving under new circumstances is Niu Shuguang, an amicable old man I first met in Tianjin in 1984. At that time, he was a retired factory worker who volunteered to teach ancient Greek to graduate students at Nankai University, and I was one of them. As we became familiar and close, he brought to me a stack of handwritten carbon-copied articles he had accumulated over many years, in which he had made numerous self-criticisms for his past belief in Christianity, clearly articulated the dialectical materialism of Marxism-Leninism-Maoism, and rebuked all religious beliefs as false consciousness and superstition. Through many conversations, I learned that he was once a well-known Protestant minister in the 1940s and 1950s, was imprisoned in the late 1950s for his faith, and later was released and assigned to a manual job at a factory. In prison and at the factory, he earnestly and scrupulously studied the writings of Marx, Engels, Lenin, Stalin, and Mao. He then declared and demonstrated repeatedly in writing that he had become "a socialist new man," an atheist. But the 1980s was a period of rapid change. When some Protestant churches were reopened in Tianjin, Niu made some strong remarks criticizing their superstitious ritual practices. His criticism sounded genuine to me. But things changed very quickly during those days. Only two or three years later, he accepted a faculty position at the Yanjing Christian Seminary in Beijing. He also reclaimed a book of New Testament exposition that he had authored in the 1940s and early 1950s, which, unbeknownst to him, had been published in Hong Kong without acknowledging the author's name. When I visited him at the seminary in Beijing a few years later, he spoke without reservation about his recovered Christian faith, as genuine as he had been since I had first got to know him. Niu is but one of many believers who once suppressed their religion under the repressive regime. Both his atheism and his recovered faith in Christ appeared to be sincere.

SEEKERS AROUND

The atheist ideology-driven regulators want to reduce religion and have repeatedly and alarmingly called attention to "religious fevers" since the early 1980s. As predicted in the economics of shortage, the phenomenon of excessive demand for religion will persist in spite of planning and effort. When visiting religious sites, it is indeed common to witness what appears to be an excessive demand for religion. Religious seekers abound, with many queuing up for the scarce religious goods and services.

For instance, overcrowded churches and temples are common scenes in today's China. During my fieldwork research since 2000, I have visited many Christian churches in coastal cities and the inland provinces. In almost all of these places, I observed churches filled beyond capacity. In Beijing, each of the churches even offered multiple Sunday services to accommodate the growing number of worshippers. When necessary, folding stools were added in the aisles of the sanctuary. Some churches had overflow rooms with closed-circuit TV sets transmitting the service from the main sanctuary. In the southern city of Guangzhou, youth services were held on Sunday afternoons. The attendance in the summer of 2000 always spilled outside, with dozens of people standing in the sun even when the temperature hovered around 100 degrees Fahrenheit. In the southwestern mountainous city of Nanchong, Sichuan, a wooden building designed to hold 400 people was packed with about 600 worshippers every Sunday before they moved to a new and larger building. In the northeastern coastal city of Dalian, one church held multiple services throughout the week. Every service was packed, with wooden pews designed for four people seating as many as six congregants and the space between rows smaller than that between economy-class seats on commercial airplanes. Many people would arrive one or two hours before the scheduled start of service in order to obtain a seat in the sanctuary. For those who arrived merely on time, it would be too late to get the preferred seat in either the sanctuary or the overflow rooms. They would have to sit on small plastic stools in the yard and listen to the choir and the sermon over loudspeakers. Tony Lambert, who visited many Protestant churches in various parts of China, reports the same—people arriving at church two hours before the service starts in order to find a seat, and at times many left standing in torrential rain while attending the service.[31]

Overcrowded conditions are not unique to Christian churches. Some Buddhist and Daoist temples have been similarly crammed beyond physical capacity during holidays and festivals. According to news releases from the China Tourism Bureau and the official Xinhua News Agency, on the Chinese New Year's Day of 2004, the Huayan Buddhist Temple in Chongqing City received more than 40,000 "incense visitors" (*xiang ke*, pilgrims), and the Lingyin Buddhist Temple near Hangzhou City received 45,100 visitors. In Shanghai, about 151,000 people visited Buddhist and Daoist temples on New Year's Eve alone. On the first six days of the Chinese New Year, the Beijing White Cloud Daoist Temple sold about 600,000 tickets to visitors.

Admittedly, holiday visitors to temples are not necessarily religious. But when better measures of religiosity are not available, temple visits may be used as a proxy measure. This proximate measure of religiousness has also been used by other scholars inside and outside China.[32] Choosing to visit a temple on New Year's Day or New Year's Eve can be considered an indicator of the visitor's priorities; the visitor could have chosen instead, for example, to visit family or friends for a dinner party. Even if the visitor was passively dragged to the temple by a friend or family member just for the "red-hot" fun (*re nao*), the exposure to religious scenes, rituals, and the atmosphere might serve to stimulate the person's interest in religion or to awaken religious hunger that had been lying dormant. Meanwhile, many people do visit the temples for what are clearly religious beliefs and practices. For example, some people squeeze hard into the temple in order to burn the "first incense sticks" (*tou xiang*) or to touch the zodiac symbols for blessings, thereby indicating supernatural beliefs instead of merely secular fun.

I observed the enthusiasm of religious seekers in Shenzhen, a coastal city near Hong Kong. Accompanied by a friend, I visited a church's weekly youth gathering on the third floor of an abandoned factory building. It was a humid and hot Friday in the summer of 2000. Later in the afternoon, rain began to pour down. Given the location of the church on this rainy evening, I expected a small turn-out. However, when I entered the large, bare-bricked hall, I was surprised to find more than 200 young people in attendance. At the church office, a woman pastor was chatting with a few first-time visitors, including myself. Within fifteen minutes before the start of the night's gathering, as I remained in the small office, the pastor received three phone calls. All were from strangers who were asking for directions to the church and were given the necessary information. And they all arrived. At the end of the gathering, some newcomers came to the office with questions. But the pastor was too busy to conduct a focused conversation with any of them. Although most of the visitors did not get their questions answered, they bought some bibles and religious books before leaving, and some told the pastor that they would return.

Ironically, the overcrowding of churches and temples itself may serve to stimulate onlookers' interest in religion. In

Dalian, I observed that some passersby became attracted by the attendance that spilled out into the churchyard. Some walked over to the sanctuary entrance for a closer look, taking a moment to listen attentively to the singing and preaching over the loudspeakers. Some attendants made friendly gestures to such onlookers by offering a stool or sharing a hymnal book or Bible. Such friendly gestures might generate curiosity for the onlookers, leading them to wonder: Why do these people do this? What do they believe? And why does believing in religion make them behave in such ways? Such curiosity may ignite a spiritual awakening. I interviewed a woman from Anhui who used to be a library clerk at a factory. When visiting Hefei, the provincial capital, she happened upon a worship service at a church near the hospital she had visited. She went in with curiosity about the devoted crowd. Followed by a series of incidents "led by God," as she described them, she converted to Christianity. Later, she became the founder of the first church at the county seat of her residence, and she went on to develop more than seventy churches throughout the county within about fifteen years.

Besides stumbling upon temples and churches, seekers also seek out the religious believers. In Guangzhou, a Christian told me about an informal book club, whose participants were young, college-educated intellectuals. They chose some books of Western culture to read and discuss. Somehow they decided to read the Bible, because it was considered one of the most important books in Western culture. However, they encountered much frustration in their discussion of the book. Eventually, they decided that they needed to find "a true and educated Christian" who could explain the true meaning of the Bible and Christian beliefs. They evolved themselves into a group of seekers ready to be evangelized. Tony Lambert also reports: "In south China, soon after the events in Beijing [the student-led democracy movement and the Tiananmen massacre in June 1989], over 200 students [who had little knowledge of Christianity] came literally knocking on the door of the local TSPM church seeking answers to their anguished questions."[33]

I even observed people queuing up for baptisms at a Christian church in Guangzhou. Inquirers were required to take a series of lessons for two months, fill out a long application form, and pass a long written exam before their applications were even considered. For those who had passed the written exam, a pastoral staff member would interview each applicant to decide whether he or she was ready to be baptized.

A waiting list for baptism was common in most of the churches I visited. My interviewees told me that sometimes these waiting lists occurred because of the lack of ordained clergymen authorized to perform baptisms. More often, it was because of quotas implicitly or explicitly imposed by the local Religious Affairs Bureau (RAB) and/or the Chinese Communist Party's United Front Department (UFD). Because of the atheist ideology and the desire to reduce religion, in a given city or county, if a religion, especially Christianity, grows too rapidly, the local RAB and UFD cadres may face reprimands or diminished chance of promotion. Consequently, local RAB/UFD cadres press local religious organizations to slow down the admission of new converts.

Ironically, the hurdles for becoming a church member may serve as a mechanism for selecting the most knowledgeable and most committed believers and disparaging free-riders who only want to take advantage of the church, consequently resulting in, on average, a higher level of commitment among the church members.[34] In turn, these church members manifest a high level of enthusiasm for evangelism and for serving as role models, inspiring seekers and prospective converts. As a result, more and more people become active in their demand for religion.

THE CHRONIC SHORTAGE OF SUPPLY

All of the demand-side dynamics described above are in response to the shortage of supply, which, under the current dominance of atheist ideology, will persist. János Kornai argues that in a shortage economy, the growth of firms is resource-constrained instead of demand-constrained.[35] Basic resources for production include the physical space, input materials, and labor. In the religious economy, the resource constraints are a result not so much of the lack of resources but of regulatory restrictions. In China's religious sector, all of these resources, namely, religious venues, religious materials, and religious labor (clergy), are under tight control and restriction by the authorities, resulting in a chronic shortage.

First, the Party-state restricts the number of venues open for religious activities. All religious buildings were closed down during the Cultural Revolution. Since 1979, a limited number of temples, mosques, and churches have been reopened for religious activities. However, the number and the process of reopening have been tightly controlled. Following Document No. 19 of 1982, the State Council published a circular in 1983 stating that the reopening of temples, in principle, should be limited to those that were used for religious activities immediately before the Cultural

Revolution.[36] The rest, if not occupied for other purposes, would remain to be treated as historical and cultural relics or tourist sites under the administration of other government agencies rather than the Religious Affairs Bureau. The implied rationale for the limited reopening of temples was that the extant religious believers were those people who had religion before the Communist liberation in 1949 and were incapable of becoming or refused to become socialist new persons; the new generations who had grown up under the red flag in new China would require no religion.

The central planning of religious sites continued in the 1990s. In 1991, a regulation specified that opening a religious site needed to be approved by county- or higher-level government authorities.[37] In 1996, a stricter restriction was imposed: "it must be approved by the provincial-level government."[38] Interestingly, the central planners at the time appeared to believe that the existing number of religious sites had been sufficient to meet the demand for religion in the population; as the 1996 circular states, "given that the existing Buddhist temples have basically met the need of believing masses for normal religious activities, in general no new temples should be constructed from now on."[39]

In reality, however, the existing religious sites have been insufficient to meet the demand that, unexpected by the regulators, has been growing. Admittedly, it is difficult to determine an optimal number of religious sites to be sufficient to meet the demand, as religious demand itself is difficult to define and probably elastic. Nevertheless, a comparison with the United States in actual supply may be indicative to some extent. On average, in 1997, there were 6.5 government-approved religious sites for every 100,000 Chinese (85,000 per 1.3 billion), whereas there are about 117 religious congregations for every 100,000 Americans (350,000 per 0.3 billion).[40] Put another way, whereas there is one church for every 857 Americans, there is one church or temple for every 15,294 people in China. The latest official Xinhua News Agency report said that in 2009, the number of religious venues had increased to 130,000, which makes it one church or temple for every 10,000 people. This is certainly impressive growth but apparently still far less than needed to meet the demand that has also been increasing. We may also take Taiwan for comparison. In 2010, the government of the Republic of China reported 15,118 temples or churches in Taiwan.[41] With a total population of 23 million, this means one church or temple for every 1,350 people. This ratio is lower than that of the United States but dramatically higher than that of the People's Republic of China. These contrasts are stark to the extreme. Even if one insists that the Chinese have never been a very religious people, whereas religious oversupply is a problem in the United States, a difference of 12 to 18 times fewer religious congregations in China is at least indicative of a certain level of shortage of religious supply. The shortage of supply is evident on the ground that almost all of the government-approved temples and churches in China are significantly overcrowded, as has been described above.

We may also look at some historical comparisons within China itself. In Shanghai, for example, the 280 Protestant churches present in 1949 were reduced to 23 by 1990, the 1950 Buddhist temples dropped to 19, the 392 Catholic churches to 43, the 236 Daoist temples to 6, and the 19 Islamic mosques to 6.[42] According to an oral briefing by a government official at a meeting in 2006, there were 375 religious sites in Shanghai in 2005, including 85 Buddhist temples, 15 Daoist temples, 7 Muslim mosques, 104 Catholic churches, and 164 Protestant churches. It is true that there has been a rapid increase in the reform era. However, the overall number has remained far less than that of the pre-PRC era. Moreover, the Chinese population has approximately tripled since 1949, from about 450 million to more than 1.3 billion today, and the increase has been even greater in the Shanghai metropolis.

Second, the Party-state restricts clergy formation. Since 1979, some religious schools or seminaries have been officially opened to train young clergy. According to the Chinese government's *White Paper: Freedom of Religious Belief in China* in 1997, by 1995, there were 32 Buddhist seminaries, 2 Daoist seminaries, 9 Islamic seminaries, 13 Catholic seminaries, and 17 Protestant seminaries. The total number of religious schools increased from 91 in 1995 to 110 in 2009.[43] Most of the seminaries have had small enrollments in the dozens or hundreds. The CCP United Front Department (UFD) and government Religious Affairs Bureau (RAB) decide which schools to open and how many seminarian students to admit. Without government approval, no organization or individual is allowed to run a seminary or train clergy.[44] The State Administration of Religious Affairs enacted the "Rules about Establishing Religious Seminaries" in December 2006. The restrictions on the seminaries have been increased.

Because of the tight control, the number of clergy remains extremely low. According to figures released by the government (see table 5.1 above), the number of Catholic priests and nuns increased from 3,400 in 1982 to 4,300 in 1995 and to 5,260 in 2009; Protestant ministers from 5,900 to 18,000, then to 37,000; Muslim imams from 20,000 to 40,000 and remained the same; Buddhist monks and nuns from

27,000 to 200,000 and remained the same; and Daoist monks and nuns from 2,600 to 25,700, then to 50,000. These are impressive increases in most of the cases. However, we have to keep in mind that the numbers of lay believers have increased even faster and that the laity/clergy ratios in the red market of religion remain very imbalanced. In 1995, there were 930 Catholics to every priest or nun, 556 Protestants to every minister, and 450 Muslims to every imam. In 2009, based on the official numbers, on average, there were 1,008 Catholics to a priest or nun, 432 Protestants to a minister, and 525 Muslims to an imam. In reality, the problem is even more acute, as the actual number of believers is definitely higher than the officially published estimates, and many older clergy have suffered both physical and psychological torture and have become too feeble to be in active service.

Third, the Party and the state restrict the publication and distribution of religious scriptures, books, and other printed materials. For example, an RAB and Police Bureau joint circular in 1988 insists: "Christian scriptures, books, and magazines must be approved by provincial-level government for printing and publishing. Only Christian organizations [approved by the government] may apply for the permit and do so according to state regulations of press. No other organizations or individuals are allowed to edit, print, or distribute Christian scriptures, books, magazines, and tracts."[45] The Amity Printing Company in Nanjing has printed tens of millions of copies of the Christian Bible, but this company holds a monopoly in the market. The distribution channel is also monopolized by the network of the government-approved Three-Self Patriotic Movement Committees. Moreover, Document No. 19 stipulates that religious scriptures, booklets, or pamphlets may not be distributed outside religious premises, even if distributed by clergy or believers of the officially approved temples, mosques, and churches.

In sum, the regulation on religious supply has been very restrictive. However, restrictive measures are not always enforceable. While religious activities, scriptures, and clergy formation are not allowed openly, some religious activities simply go underground. Foreigners have smuggled Bibles and religious publications into China. The control apparatus has been rounding up "self-designated evangelists" or ministers without government recognition (*zi feng chuan dao ren*), but such evangelists continue to rise up and proselytize. Some sects, such as the Christianity-inspired Shouters, have experienced crackdowns since the early 1980s, but they still persist, spread, and mutate in organizational form. The black and gray markets of religion exist because of the shortage of supply under very restrictive regulations.

BALANCING DEMAND AND SUPPLY

To respond to the perceived "excessive demand," regulators have three available options. The first is to reduce the active demand, that is, the people's expressed desire for the goods and services, through education. The Party-state has tried hard to intensify the education and propaganda of atheism, including creating a new magazine, *Science and Atheism,* in 1999 and instituting curriculum and extracurricular programs in schools. However, atheist propaganda has become less effective in the reform era, while more people's spiritual hunger is awakened. Meanwhile, as more foreigners visit and work in China and more Chinese visit, study, and live in the

West, religious freedom has become ever more consciously accepted by the Chinese citizens.

The second option is to raise the costs for the desired goods and services. The Communist authorities have tried hard to accomplish this by imposing more restrictive regulations and tightening the control over religious groups. However, economic reforms and opening up toward the world make it difficult and ineffective for Chinese authorities to raise the costs of practicing religion. Following the standards of the United Nations, religious freedom has been inscribed in the PRC Constitution, and the reform-minded leaders in the CCP have promoted the rule of law to some extent. Some international nongovernmental organizations serve as watchdogs of human-rights violations in China. The United States, some other Western governments, and some United Nations agencies openly criticize the Chinese government's violations of religious freedom and other human rights. Moreover, raising financial and social costs for religious believers will not only draw criticism but may also retard foreign investment in China.

In reality, the social costs of practicing religion have been practically reduced in the reform era, as the social control mechanisms have been substantially altered along with the economic market transition. The "People's Communes" in the rural areas have been transformed into townships. *Danwei* (work units) in the urban areas have lost some of their functions. Even the Chinese Communist Party, supposedly the party of the proletariat, has opened its membership to businessmen and entrepreneurs. In this social context, practicing religion has become increasingly tolerated, accepted, and appreciated by the residents within society.

The third option is to increase religious supply. As a matter of fact, the Chinese authorities have been accommodating in this regard, allowing more temples to be restored and more churches built. However, by taking the organizational threat seriously, the Party-state has been trying hard not to lose control over the apparently inevitable growth of religion. On the one hand, some official measures have been taken to promote Buddhism and folk religion to counterbalance the growth of Catholicism and Protestantism. In 2006 and 2009, the government sponsored two World Buddhist Forums. In 2007, it sponsored the International Daodejing Forum. Traditional communal religions (folk religion) have been restored in many places in the name of preserving non-material cultural heritage. But such measures have also triggered consciousness of competition among leaders and lay believers of the religions. The new paradigm of the sociology of religion maintains that competition tends to increase religious participation. Therefore, such measures to increase the supply of some religions have played into the invisible hand of the market force for greater religious competition, resulting in increased demand for religion.

On the other hand, the authorities have been striving for more effective planning of religious venues. In Shanghai, for example, the United Front Department and the Religious Affairs Bureau commissioned research projects of religious venues and religious believers in the city, with the intention of making "rational placement of religious venues" (*heli buju*). Such a stereotypical practice of the central-planning economy has now been applied to religion. However, such central planning, just as in the material economy, inevitably leads to a chronic shortage of supply and is bound to fail in terms of meeting people's varied and changing needs for religion, not to mention the fact that this inevitably involves the state in decisions about which religious groups are to be given preference.[46] In Shanghai, which is undergoing an active central planning of religious sites, the government-approved churches continue to be overcrowded, and nonregistered churches continue to exist and grow, while the banned religious sects continue to operate, despite frequent raids and punishments.

CONCLUSION

The description and discussion above show that political factors in the religious economy are very important. The socialist religious economy based on atheist Communist ideology is by nature a shortage economy, in which the religious demand is far from stable. Eradication measures failed to wipe out religion from society during the Cultural Revolution, and restrictive regulations have failed to contain religion in reform-era China. While the Communists have tried hard to force upon the people the atheist Communist ideology, many individuals have sought solace in alternative spiritualities without a religious label, that is, semi-, quasi- or pseudo-religious beliefs and practices. Even though the authorities have tried hard to spell out regulatory procedures, carry out periodical crackdowns on various religious groups and activities, and severely punish the leaders of banned religious movements, the dormant religious need has been awakened, and the active demand for religion has kept growing throughout the reform era. The growing demand in turn stimulates religious supply and forces the authorities to adapt their regulation and enforcement strategies.

Without deregulation, the problem of seemingly "excessive demand" for religion, or the shortage of the supply of religion, will not abate in China. The political-economic approach identifies the central role of ideology in China's religious regulation strategy. The shortage of religious supply is not only a problem of central planning but is also driven by the atheist ideology. As long as atheism is maintained as part of ideological orthodoxy, changes in religion policy will be no more than cosmetic, and the shortage economy of religion will persist.

OLIGOPOLY DYNAMICS:

CHINA AND BEYOND

THE PREVIOUS CHAPTERS have provided descriptions and analysis of religion in China. In this concluding chapter, besides summarizing the main theoretical arguments, I would like to point out that China is not unique in terms of religious regulation and its unintended consequences. What we have learned in examining the China case may be extended to analyze religion in some other countries, although modifications may be necessary for analyzing a particular case.

In short, this study adopts a political-economic approach to explain the survival and revival of religion in China. It explains that despite restrictive regulations that are driven by the atheist ideology, religion has been reviving throughout China. It argues that the Chinese religious economy under Communist rule is a shortage economy, where religious supply is heavily regulated, religious demand is vivaciously dynamic, and religious regulations are rendered ineffective because of the "invisible hand" of market forces or economic laws. The shortage of religious supply under heavy regulation inevitably results in the triple religious markets: the red, black, and gray markets of religion.

The triple religious market model is not a Chinese paradigm, as R. Stephen Warner suggested (see chapter 1 above). Rather, it is a model probably common to most of the religious markets under heavy regulation. Looking around the world today, we find that most countries maintain certain level of restrictive regulations over religion.[1] The polarizing models of religious monopoly and religious pluralism have dominated the existing literature of sociological studies of church-state relations. But in the actual world today, the predominant type of church-state relations is neither pluralism nor monopoly but, rather, oligopoly, where only a select few religions are legal, while the rest of the religious groups have to operate in the underground or the gray areas of the law. The triple religious market model developed in examining the Chinese case may be applicable to examining other oligopoly societies.

THE TRIPLE RELIGIOUS MARKETS IN OTHER SOCIETIES

First, the triple religious markets have existed in countries of the former Soviet societies. Although the Soviet world in Europe has collapsed, the social experiments by the Soviets should not be forgotten. Most studies of religion in the Soviet Union have focused on government-sanctioned churches (the red market) and/or underground groups (the black market). These studies have shown the dynamics of the two markets. For example, "The closure of monasteries led to the phenomenon of 'monasteries without walls' and 'monasticism in the world.'"[2] In 1963, the Council for the Affairs of Religious Cults claimed to have successfully reduced the number of Muslim communities, Old Believers, and Baptists but also admitted that the number of illegal synagogues, Roman Catholic, and Lutheran churches increased. In addition, there were illegal sects, including Pentecostals, Jehovah's Witnesses, and True Orthodox. John Anderson says: "Clearly, in this area the state enjoyed limited success, with even the reported reductions perhaps hiding the continuing extent of the problem. Indeed, official policies during these years may have compounded the problem, for the deprivation of registration did not guarantee the death of a congregation."[3]

This is insightful about the limited effectiveness of state efforts to suppress religion. However, without the conceptual tool of the gray market, groups and activities with ambiguous legal status have been largely neglected in the studies of religion in the Soviet Union. But, on separate accounts, it is also known that shamanism existed as a form of ethnic culture, and this and other popular religious practices persisted in the former Soviet Union.[4] Other types of gray-market religions also existed, especially in the form of the personality cults of Lenin and Stalin. Given that the red market was heavily restricted and the black market was suppressed in the Soviet Union, as the theories of shortage economy and triple markets of religion would predict, there must have been a substantially large gray market of religion in Soviet society. More focused historical research is needed to verify or falsify this theory-driven hypothesis for the Soviet Union.

The Communist government of Poland maintained probably the least restrictive religious regulation in the Soviet bloc. The majority of the population remained as openly active Catholics throughout the period of Communist rule. Correspondingly, the black market was small, with perhaps only a few illegally organized Catholic groups from time to time and a small number of Catholics who openly dissented from the "patriotic priests" and "regime Catholics." Nevertheless, a gray market existed. Catholics carried out activities that the government found objectionable and tried to suppress, such as popular devotions to the Black Madonna, pilgrimages to shrines, and "the Great Novena of the Millennium" festivities.[5]

Second, the triple religious markets evidently exist in non-Communist East Asian societies. Religion in Taiwan was heavily regulated until 1987 under the authoritarian regime of the Chinese Nationalist Party (*Kuomintang* or *Guomindang*). There was an open market of government-sanctioned religions (we might use the color of white or blue to represent it), a black market of government-suppressed religions, and a large gray market of folk religion and spiritualities.[6] In the white or blue market, there were government-approved associations of Buddhists, Protestants, and Catholics. In the black market, Yiguan Dao was one of the banned religions that persisted and increased despite suppression.[7] Pre–World War II Japan and South Korea under the authoritarian regimes also imposed heavy regulation on religion. Both societies became fertile fields that bred numerous new religious or spiritual movements that spread beyond their borders.[8]

Finally, the triple religious markets also exist in non-Communist and non-Asian societies. In medieval Europe, besides the monopolistic Roman Catholic church (the open market that might be referred to with the color cardinal red) and the suppressed heretic groups (the black market), there were widespread popular religious practices that contained pagan elements, toward which the official church and the state held uneasy positions (the gray market). In addition, there was Judaism, which was variably suppressed or tolerated. Overall, the gray market might not have been very small. Similar phenomena can be found in modern South America, where the majority of the population are nominal Catholics but indigenous and/or heretical groups are widespread. A gray market may exist even in the United States, where nonconventional religions are making inroads in the form of "health cults," such as through yoga and meditation centers, or in the form of "ethnic culture." As an example of the latter, since 1997, immigrant Buddhists in Houston have celebrated *Vesak*, the Buddha's birthday, largely as an immigrant cultural fiesta, during which a concert of Buddhist music is held at a university to introduce Buddhism to the nonimmigrant public.[9] The spectators and some of the participants may take it merely as cultural instead of religious, but the core leaders and many participants are religious believers who take pride in the opportunity to introduce Buddhism to the larger public. They hope that the festival celebration may help to draw some Americans into Buddhism, or at least it may improve the relationship between the Buddhist religion and the American culture at large.

FOUR TYPES OF STATE-RELIGION RELATIONS

In the study of religious change in European and American societies, the contrasting models of religious monopoly and pluralism have been the main axis of theoretical constructions.[10] However, the dominant type of church-state relations in the world today is neither monopoly nor pluralism but oligopoly, the dominance of a select few religions in a society.

There have been four types of state-religion relations in human history: religious monopoly, pluralism, oligopoly, and the total ban of religion by the state. Many countries, including China, have never had a religious monopoly or pluralism. Instead, they have maintained religious oligopoly. In religious oligopoly, the state allows more than one religion to operate legally, but other religions are banned and subject to repression.[11] China is an example of religious oligopoly par excellence. For millennia, there have been multiple religions allowed to operate, yet the government has maintained restrictive regulations on these religions and suppressed heterodox or sectarian religious movements.[12] Under Communist rule since 1949, China officially allows only five religions: Buddhism, Daoism, Islam, Catholicism, and Protestant Christianity. But China is not the only country that maintains religious oligopoly. In Indonesia, the Ministry of Religious Affairs extends official status to six religious groups: Islam, Catholicism, Protestantism, Buddhism, Hinduism, and Confucianism. Iran recognizes Islam, and the Constitution states that "within the limits of the law," Zoroastrians, Jews, and Christians are the only recognized religious minorities guaranteed freedom to practice their religious beliefs. Indeed, oligopoly is the most prevalent type in the world today, as table 7.1 shows.

In addition, China once imposed a total ban on religion, as described in chapter 4 above. All churches, temples, and mosques were closed down during the Cultural Revolution. The Maoists tried hard to eradicate religion and substitute for it an atheist ideology. A total ban on religion has happened rarely but not uniquely. As far as I know, at least one other country once banned all religions: Albania under the Communists.[13] The Soviet Union and other Communist

Table 7.1

FOUR TYPES OF STATE-RELIGION RELATIONS

"To what extent is there a favored (or established) religion in the country?"

Religious policy/law		Number of countries	Percent
Pluralism	All religious brands are treated the same	40	20.4
	Cultural or historical legacies only	16	8.2
Oligopoly	Some brands have special privileges or government access	56	28.6
Monopoly	One religious brand has privileges or government access	41	20.9
	One single state or official religious brand	43	21.9
Total Ban	All religions are banned	(2)	
TOTAL		196	100.0

Note: "Cross-National Data: Religion Indexes, Religious Adherents, and Other Data" (http://www.thearda.com/). This file assembles data from multiple sources, but many of the measures are from the Association of Religion Data Archives' coding of the 2003 U.S. State Department's International Religious Freedom Reports. This coding produced data on 195 different countries and territories (see Grim and Finke, "International Religious Indexes," for a list of countries coded) but excluded the United States. Additional data on religious regulation and favoritism in the smaller countries not covered by the State Department reports were provided by researchers at the World Christian Database. In addition, this project assembled (with permission) other cross-national measures of interest to researchers on religion, economics, and politics. They include adherent information from the World Christian Database, scales from Freedom House and the Heritage Foundation, and various socioeconomic measures from the United Nations. Measures for religious persecution (AESTIMA) and ethnic identity (DETHNIC) were added to this file in August 2007.

countries had at least some churches, mosques, or temples open for religious activities throughout the Communist-ruled era. To my knowledge, a total ban on religion is not practiced in any country today. Nevertheless, it is an important type for the full understanding of church-state relations. The failures of such experiments in China and Albania may have implications for various secularist experiments in other societies.

If we look at it from the perspective of the state, the differences between the total ban and pluralism may be regarded as quantitative—banning all, banning all but one, banning all but a few, or banning none. Evidently, many countries in the world today grant legal status to only a selected few religions. Brian Grim and Roger Finke compiled a "Cross-National Data" that includes a question about state-religion relations: "To what extent is there a favored (or established) religion in the country?"[14] The left column of table 7.1 is my categorization of the four major types. The table shows that about 20 percent of the countries are pluralistic, and slightly more countries are monopolistic. The majority of the countries, almost 58 percent, are more or less oligopolistic. Even if we adopt a stricter criterion of formal regulations, about 50 percent of the countries in the world today still remain oligopolistic. This global fact of religious oligopoly makes it necessary to rethink and reconstruct theories of church-state relations and religious change within society.

PLURALISM, PLURALITY, AND PLURALIZATION

In the sociology of religion, there have been ongoing debates about religious pluralism, including the heated debates on the relationship between religious pluralism and religious vitality. The old wisdom, known as the secularization theory, was that religious pluralism would lead to religious decline because it undermines the plausibility of religion.[15] In contrast, "new paradigm" scholars argue that religious pluralism is associated with religious vitality because it bolsters competition among religious groups.[16] While the negative correlation between religious pluralism and religious vitality has been rejected by most scholars, including Peter Berger,[17] the positive correlation between religious pluralism and religious participation has been subject to fierce dispute.[18] This debate has involved painstaking technicalities of measurements and statistical procedures. However, so far, the involved scholars have made little effort to clarify the concept of pluralism itself. What is pluralism? Is it accidental or inevitable?

As a step toward clarification, it is necessary to distinguish the descriptive and normative uses of the term *pluralism*. James A. Beckford suggests using "diversity" for the former and "pluralism" for the latter.[19] Robert Wuthnow substantiates these distinctions succinctly in his 2003 presidential address to the Society for the Scientific Study of Religion: "If diversity is concerned descriptively with the degree of heterogeneity among units within a society, pluralism refers to the normative evaluation of this diversity and with the social arrangements put in place to maintain these normative judgments."[20] In light of this distinction, the above-mentioned dispute appears to surround the descriptive diversity. However, the persisting use of *pluralism* instead of *diversity* indicates that the involved scholars might hold, consciously or unconsciously, to a normative position: They regard pluralism as either a good thing or a bad thing and thus argue for its positive effect on religious vitality or the lack of it, respectively.

The descriptive and normative dimensions of pluralism may indeed be entangled, so much so that adopting two seemingly unrelated terms may not be the best approach for conceptualization and theorizing. Following the lead of some scholars,[21] I would adopt a set of related words with the same root—*plurality, pluralization,* and *pluralism*—to define the interconnected status, process, and configuration on the *social* level:

> Plurality (diversity) describes the *status* or *degree* of religious heterogeneity within a society.
> Pluralization is the *process* of increasing plurality within a society.
> Pluralism refers to the *social arrangements* favorable to a high or increased level of plurality.

I would further differentiate "social arrangements" of pluralism into legal, civic, and cultural arrangements. The pluralistic legal structure that legitimizes religious freedom is favorable to increased plurality. In modern times, the legal structure appears to be the key to pluralization, or the lack of it. On the other hand, most existing religions seem to have a natural tendency to seek a monopoly in society, attempting to ally with state powers whenever possible to achieve and maintain a monopoly. Without the intellectual understanding and certain level of social consensus that legitimize and justify an individual freedom of religion and group equality of religions, without civic organizations in the civil society that keep in check and balance the state agencies and religious organizations, the pluralistic legal structure cannot be implemented or maintained in practice. Therefore, the civic and cultural arrangements are foundational to attain and retain the legal arrangement for pluralism.

It is important to keep in mind that pluralism has also been used to refer to a position on the individual level, a philosophical or theological position regarding the relationship between one's own religion and other religions. Besides pluralism, other philosophical or theological positions include relativism, exclusivism, and inclusivism.[22] Robert Wuthnow distinguishes individual and social pluralism this way: "A pluralist [person] is someone who can see and appreciate all points of view, a person who is presumably tolerant, informed, cosmopolitan, and a pluralist society is one in which social arrangements favor the expression of diverse perspectives and lifestyles."[23] We may call these individual pluralism and social pluralism, respectively. The problem of secularization theory, especially in the form articulated by Peter Berger in the 1960s, is that it confuses individual pluralism and social pluralism. Empirical evidence has shown that the social arrangements of religious pluralism do not necessarily lead to individual pluralism or relativism. For example, in the United States and many other pluralistic societies, there are many fundamentalists who squarely reject theological or philosophical pluralism. In the meantime, many of these people affirm the social pluralism that guarantees their freedom of religious belief and practice. Therefore, the pluralistic society in reality has created sufficient social space for individuals to choose and hold on to one of the philosophical/theological positions or attitudes. Social pluralism is the focus in this chapter.

Applying this set of social-level descriptive terms in the world today, we may begin with these propositions regarding the relationship between religion and society in modern times:

1. Religious pluralization is the general trend in modern societies.
2. More and more states have adopted the legal arrangement for religious pluralism.
3. In a given society, the civic and cultural arrangements of religious pluralism tend to lag behind the adoption of the pluralistic legal arrangement.

Pluralization happens in many societies but is more common in the modern world. A tribal or relatively isolated society may maintain a substantial level of religious homogeneity. However, modern economic, political, and social changes and structures have created spiritual and intellectual conditions favorable to pluralization, which takes place either through the invention of new sects (denominations) or through importation of foreign religions. Globalization further increases the interconnectedness of societies and eases religious diffusion across the world. In the globalizing world, people of different religious traditions become neighbors, either physically through migration or virtually through the mass media and the Internet.

Modernization and globalization under the influence of liberal democratic principles that originated in the modern West have resulted in the adoption of the pluralistic legal arrangement by an increasing number of countries. However, the intellectual understanding of this pluralism remains limited in most societies, resulting in the lack of civic and cultural arrangements for religious pluralism. The Pew Forum on Religion and Public Life's report on *Global Restrictions on Religion*[24] distinguishes government restrictions and social hostilities to plural religions. The two indexes tend to move together (positively correlated); that is, higher scores on one index generally are associated with higher scores on the other.

Historically speaking, the United Nations "Universal Declaration of Human Rights" in 1948 may have promoted the adoption of religious freedom in the constitution or basic law of the member countries of the United Nations. On December 10, 1948, the General Assembly of the United Nations adopted and proclaimed the "Universal Declaration of Human Rights." Following this historic act, the General Assembly called upon all member countries to publicize the text of the Declaration and "to cause it to be disseminated, displayed, read and expounded principally in schools and other educational institutions, without distinction based on the political status of countries or territories." Article 18 of the Declaration states: "Everyone has the right to freedom of thought, conscience and religion; this right includes freedom to change his religion or belief, and freedom, either alone or in community with others and in public or private, to manifest his religion or belief in teaching, practice, worship and observance."

However, the adoption of religious freedom in the constitution or basic law may not come together with the shared understanding of religious freedom by the majority of citizens, nor does the underdeveloped civil society provide the necessary social and cultural support for upholding this principle. While some people strive for pluralism, others try hard to resist it or sabotage it. However, if pluralization is indeed the general trend of development, the resistance stands to lose over time. To gain a better understanding of the trend of pluralization, we need to turn to the historical development.

ACCIDENTAL AND DELIBERATE PLURALISM

An important trigger of pluralization in modern times is the separation of church and state, an innovation first experimented with in the United States. After the thirteen colonies joined to form the United States of America, the First Amendment to the Constitution was ratified in 1791. Regarding religion, it states: "Congress shall make no law respecting an establishment of religion, or prohibiting the free exercise thereof."

This legal arrangement of religious freedom includes disestablishment (no state religion) and deregulation (no prohibition of any religion). It might have happened accidentally because of the unusual religious and cultural conditions in those colonies/states at the time: "The thirteen colonies which formed the United States were populated with settlers from Western Europe (and slaves from Africa) adhering to several different religions.... Although the vast majority were Protestant Christians, they belonged to different denominations which were not at all united. Therefore, all the religions were minority religions; no one dominated."[25] Up to 1791, most of the colonies had an established church or a privileged Protestant denomination, but none of them was acceptable as the established church in the other states of the new nation. In this sense, the American experiment of the separation of church and state was accidental. It took almost fifty years before "the last traces of privilege of the Congregational Church disappeared in the state of Massachusetts."[26]

This pluralistic legal arrangement propelled the trend of pluralization in the United States. While the denominations at the founding of the country have persisted, a number of Protestant sects arrived from other countries or emerged inside. On the other hand, the new nation was very much Protestant Christian in its collective conscience, although it was a secular state in legal or legislative terms. It took about a hundred years before the United States faced the first real challenges of pluralism. That was when the south, central and east European immigrants arrived in large numbers around the turn of the twentieth century, and among them many were Catholics, Jews, and some Orthodox Christians. This substantial pluralization challenged the nation to redefine its collective identity. It took about half a century for Americans to come to terms with this new plurality. While the state maintained the pluralistic legal structure, the nation settled for the Judeo-Christian cultural identity, as is well illustrated in Will Herberg's seminal work titled *Protestant-Catholic-Jew.*[27]

Since the 1960s, the United States has been facing greater challenges of pluralism. First, amid the social turmoil and problems of race, ethnicity, gender, the Vietnam war, political ideology, and so on, numerous new religious movements emerged and attracted many young people. Social reactions to the new religious movements include the anticult and deprogramming frenzy. Second, the post-1965 new immigrants have come from Latin America, Asia, and the Mideast. Not only they are viewed as racially different, but many have brought even more different religions, including Hinduism, Buddhism, Islam, and a number of others.[28] Consequently, it is probably not an exaggeration to say that any religion that has ever existed elsewhere in the world has followers or practitioners in the United States today. The increasing presence of non-Judeo-Christian and nonconventional religions has brought many challenges to American society, among which is the burning question about national identity, as squarely raised by political scientist Samuel Huntington in *Who Are We? The Challenges to American National Identity.*[29]

Responding to these new challenges, some people have called to enlarge the inclusion by talking of "Abrahamic religions" or "one nation under God," while others have contested for the Protestant Christian roots of the nation. Meanwhile, many people come to reexamine the very notion of pluralism. Is pluralism a good thing for American society? Although some scholars have championed it,[30] others have sounded more cautious.[31] Some legal cases and political contentions have challenged the pluralistic legal arrangement itself. Worrying about this ongoing trial of pluralism, some scholars argue that "disestablishment and protection of religious freedom are never permanent. In the United States, they remain in danger of being overturned at any time by those with particular religious beliefs."[32] It is a dynamic balance indeed. In my view, however, because the civil and cultural arrangements of pluralism are in place, and because civil society is well developed in the United States, the overturning of the legal separation of state and religion is unlikely to happen. Pluralization seems irreversible.

Even though the innovative experiment of pluralism started accidentally, the idea of church-state separation seems infectious, just as innovations have a natural tendency of diffusion.[33] Of course, the diffusion of state-religion separation has been a long and painful process, full of challenges, twists, and turns, as many European and Asian countries exhibit.

China is an interesting case in this regard. For centuries, multiple religions existed in imperial China. Confucianism, a cultural tradition that has a religious dimension or is quasi-religious, had been the orthodoxy, whereas Daoist and

Buddhist sects existed alongside as supplementary hetero-doxies.[34] Following the revolution in 1911 that overthrew the imperial Qing Dynasty, China became the first republic in Asia. Around that time, facing Western imperialism and the pressure to construct the modern nation-state, some Chinese elites considered establishing Confucianism as the monopolistic national religion or state religion (*guo jiao*), as the Britons did with Anglicanism or the Japanese with Shinto. After fierce debates and struggles, the American model eventually prevailed. The new Republic of China adopted the principle of religious freedom in its constitution, even though there was a lack of shared understanding among the populace and the elites. In the following decades, wars and political turmoil destabilized China. Eventually, the Chinese Communist Party took power in mainland China in 1949. The Republic of China under Kuomintang (the Nationalist Party) withdrew to the island of Taiwan and imposed martial law for almost four decades. Only after the lifting of martial law in 1987 did the freedom of religion in the Constitution of the Republic of China become practiced. Today, many religions and religious groups or sects freely operate in Taiwan. In mainland China, the freedom of religious belief has been retained in the Constitution of the People's Republic of China in spite of frequent political turmoil. In practice, however, various religions have been subjected to repression and eradication, as described and analyzed in previous chapters.

OLIGOPOLY DYNAMICS

In the study of church-state relations and religious change in society, the dominant sociological theories are based on

European and American experiences. When such theories are applied to non-Western societies without modification, distorted panoramas are inevitable. Given the prevalence of the religious oligopoly in the modern world, we have to adopt the lenses of oligopoly to examine the dynamics of church-state relations and religious change in society in the world today.

Let us take one example to illustrate the necessity to make conceptual adjustment or improvement. According to Stark and Finke,[35] a religious monopoly breeds a lazy clergy and, consequently, a less religiously mobilized population. In contrast, a deregulated religious economy "will tend to be very pluralistic," one in which more religious "firms" compete for a share of the market.[36] They assert, "To the degree that religious economies are unregulated and competitive, overall levels of religious participation will be high."[37] Religious change in the United States appears to provide strong evidence of deregulation effects. Since the First Amendment to the U.S. Constitution, the rate of religious adherence in the U.S. population steadily increased from 17 percent in 1774 to 62 percent in 1990.[38]

However, oligopoly economies are both regulated and competitive. There is competition among the government-sanctioned religions, but the competition is somewhat different in kind from that in pluralistic societies.[39] A strong factor in the growth of certain religious groups seems to be government favoritism, and competition for such political favoritism is common.[40] Meanwhile, religious leaders nonetheless need to mobilize other resources to succeed in the marketplace, as they are in competition with other officially sanctioned religions and also with nonsanctioned religious groups.

Therefore, an important modification to the proposition is necessary, as articulated in chapter 5 above. Increasing

restrictive regulations in oligopoly does not necessarily lead
to the decline of overall religious participation. Rather, heavy
regulation leads to complication of the religious market,
resulting in a tripartite market with distinct dynamics. Under
increased religious regulation, although participation in
formal religious organizations may decline, other forms of
religiosity will persist. To the extent that religious organizations are restricted in number and in operation, a black
market will emerge in spite of the high costs to individual
believers. To the extent that a red or open market is restricted
and a black market is suppressed, a gray market will emerge.
The gray market is made up of various explicit religious
exchanges and implicit forms of religion. The more restrictive
and suppressive the regulation, the larger the gray market
grows. Under heavy regulation, the gray market is likely to be
volatile and unsettled, making religious regulation an
arduous task and impossible to enforce by the government
superstructure.

Furthermore, in oligopoly, religious pluralization is
probably inevitable, even though it may be a slow and difficult process. Weighing the social and political benefits of religious restrictions and their financial, political, and human
costs, a rational choice on the part of the state is to relax
restrictions and grant legal status to more religions. In China,
in addition to the five major religions recognized by the
central government, some local governments have begun to
legalize certain minor religions in recent years, including
Orthodox Christianity in the northeastern province of
Heilongjiang, Mazu and Three in One in the southeastern
province of Fujian, and Huangdaxian in the southern provinces of Zhejiang and Guangdong. A number of ethnic
minority groups have reclaimed their traditional popular

religions as their distinct cultural markers. Meanwhile, various new religions that originated abroad, including Mormonism, the Unification Church, and Baha'i, have also been working to gain official recognition. In addition, some religious groups operating in the black market are trying to move to the gray market, and those in the gray market are trying to move to the red market by registering with the government.

CONCLUSION

How much can the state control religion through regulation? Obviously, the efficacy of state power has been exaggerated in regard both to Western societies and to China. The triple-market theory shows that market forces are at work, and religious groups and believers may not respond in ways that the regulators want. In the globalizing modern times, heavy regulation cannot effectively reduce religion. It can only complicate the religious market by pushing religious organizations and believers into the black and gray markets.

This study shows that it is insufficient to explain the complexity of religious dynamics in oligopolistic society by simply adopting the propositions of free-market economics. It is necessary to adopt a political-economic approach, which has been called for by some sociologists,[41] but so far, there have been few theory-driven empirical studies.

There are other important questions about religious oligopoly that should be studied. Given the prevalence of religious oligopoly in the world today, we must examine the justifications for it. Is social pluralism necessarily a good thing? Could oligopoly be a better configuration in state-religion relations? What are the most important arguments and counterarguments regarding maintaining an oligopoly that privileges one dominant religion?

In China today, there are discussions within certain elite circles about making up a state religion, perhaps something based on Confucianism, to take the place of the failing Communist ideology and maintain social cohesion. There are also discussions about preserving Chinese cultural traditions against the "foreign" religions of Christianity and Islam. A strong motivation for such suggestions is to preserve the distinct Chinese culture and nourish the Chinese national identity amid rapid globalization and Westernization. Similar arguments may be found in Russia and other countries that face the same challenges of globalization and the hegemonic Western culture.

To take a detached, scientific approach, we may ask: Is oligopoly a necessary stage toward pluralism? What does it take to pass through this stage? There are ample historical and contemporary cases for us to work on in order to achieve a better understanding of oligopoly dynamics. Such theory-driven empirical studies will have important practical implications, as well as theoretical significance.

NOTES

Preface

1. Max Weber, *The Protestant Ethic and the Spirit of Capitalism* (New York: Scribner's, 1958); also see Max Weber, *The Religion of China* (New York: Free Press, 1951).
2. Donald MacInnis, "The Secular Vision of a New Humanity in People's China," *Christian Century* (March 12, 1974): 249–253.
3. An abbreviated Chinese version of the thesis was published. Fenggang Yang, "The Change of the Notion of God in Western Philosophy," *Nankai Journal*, no. 1 (1988): 34–39.
4. Dean R. Hoge (1937–2008) published twenty-five books about religious life in America, with special focus on American Catholics and mainline Protestants. He was elected president of the Society for the Scientific Study of Religion in 2007, and he passed away on September 13, 2008.
5. My dissertation-turned-book is Fenggang Yang, *Chinese Christians in America: Conversion, Assimilation, and Adhesive Identities* (University Park, Pa.: Penn State University Press, 1999). I have coedited, with Joseph Tamney, a special issue of *Sociology of Religion* 67 (2006) focusing on "Conversion to Christianity among the Chinese" and coauthored, also with

Joseph Tamney, "Exploring Mass Conversion to Christianity among the Chinese: An Introduction" for this special issue. Another related article is Fenggang Yang, "Lost in the Market, Saved at McDonald's: Conversion to Christianity in Urban China," *Journal for the Scientific Study of Religion* 44 (2005): 423–441.

6. Some of my publications in this field include Fenggang Yang and Helen Rose Ebaugh, "Transformations in New Immigrant Religions and Their Global Implications," *American Sociological Review* 66 (2001): 269–288; Fenggang Yang and Helen Rose Ebaugh, "Religion and Ethnicity among New Immigrants: The Impact of Majority/Minority Status in Home and Host Countries," *Journal for the Scientific Study of Religion* 40 (2001): 367–378; Tony Carnes and Fenggang Yang, eds., *Asian American Religions: The Making and Remaking of Borders and Boundaries* (New York: New York University Press, 2004).

7. Quoted in C. K. Yang, *Religion in Chinese Society* (Berkeley and Los Angeles: University of California Press, 1961), 5.

8. See Yang, *Religion in Chinese Society*; also see Hans Küng and Julia Ching, *Christianity and Chinese Religions* (New York: Doubleday, 1989).

9. Yang, *Religion in Chinese Society*, 6.

10. For example, Alan Hunter and Kim-Kwong Chan, *Protestantism in Contemporary China* (Cambridge, U.K.: Cambridge University Press, 1993); Richard Madsen, *China's Catholics: Tragedy and Hope in an Emerging Civil Society* (Los Angeles and Berkeley: University of California Press, 1998).

Chapter 1

1. Andrew Greeley, "A Religious Revival in Russia?" *Journal for the Scientific Study of Religion* 33, no. 3 (1994): 253–272; Mary L. Gautier, "Church Attendance and Religious Belief in Postcommunist Societies," *Journal for the Scientific Study of Religion* 36, no. 2 (1997): 289–297; Paul Froese, "Hungary for Religion: A Supply-Side Interpretation of the Hungarian

Religious Revival," *Journal for the Scientific Study of Religion* 40, no. 2 (2001): 251–268; Paul Froese, "After Atheism: An Analysis of Religious Monopolies in the Post-Communist World," *Sociology of Religion* 65, no. 1 (2004): 57–75; Paul Froese, "Forced Secularization in Soviet Russia: Why an Atheistic Monopoly Failed," *Journal for the Scientific Study of Religion* 43, no. 1 (2004): 35–50.

2. Paul Froese and Steven Pfaff, "Replete and Desolate Markets: Poland, East Germany, and the New Religious Paradigm," *Social Forces* 80, no. 2 (2001): 481–507.

3. Peter Berger, *The Sacred Canopy: Elements of a Sociological Theory of Religion* (Garden City, N.Y.: Doubleday, 1967).

4. Peter Berger, "A Bleak Outlook Is Seen for Religion," *New York Times*, April 25, 1968, quoted in Rodney Stark, "Secularization, R.I.P.," *Sociology of Religion* 60 (1999): 249–273.

5. See "Is God Dead?" *Time*, April 8, 1966.

6. David Martin, *On Secularization: Towards A Revised General Theory* (Aldershot, U .K.: Ashgate, 2005), 19.

7. Ibid., 18.

8. Ibid.

9. Dean M. Kelly, *Why Conservative Churches Are Growing* (New York: Harper & Row, 1972); Dean R. Hoge and David A. Roozen, eds., *Understanding Church Growth and Decline: 1950–1978* (New York: Pilgrim, 1979); D. A. Roozen and C. K. Hadaway, eds., *Church and Denominational Growth* (Nashville, Tenn.: Abingdon, 1993).

10. Dean R. Hoge, *Converts, Dropouts, Returnees: A Study of Religious Change among Catholics* (New York: Pilgrim, 1981); M. Musick and J. Wilson, "Religious Switching for Marriage Reasons," *Sociology of Religion* 56 (1995): 257–270; F. Newport, "The Religious Switchers in the United States," *American Sociological Review* 44 (1979): 528–552; W. C. Roof and C. K. Hadaway, "Denominational Switching: Going beyond Stark and Glock," *Journal for the Scientific Study of Religion* 18 (1979): 363–379.

11. Andrew M. Greeley, *Religious Change in America* (Cambridge, Mass.: Harvard University Press, 1989).

12. Roger Finke and Rodney Stark, *The Churching of America, 1776–1990: Winners and Losers in Our Religious Economy* (New Brunswick, N.J.: Rutgers University Press, 1992).

13. José Casanova, *Public Religions in the Modern World* (Chicago: University of Chicago Press, 1994).

14. R. Stephen Warner, "Work in Progress toward a New Paradigm for the Sociological Study of Religion in the United States," *American Journal of Sociology* 98 (1993): 1044–1093.

15. For example, Frank J. Lechner, "The 'New Paradigm' in the Sociology of Religion: Comment on Warner," *American Journal of Sociology* 103 (1997): 182–191; R. Stephen Warner, "A Paradigm Is Not a Theory: Reply to Lechner," *American Journal of Sociology* 103 (1997): 192–199; Lawrence Young, ed., *Rational Choice Theory and Religion: Summary and Assessment* (New York: Routledge, 1997); Ted G. Jelen, ed., *Sacred Markets, Sacred Canopies: Essays on Religious Markets and Religious Pluralism* (Lanham, Md.: Rowman & Littlefield, 2003).

16. R. Stephen Warner, "More Progress on the New Paradigm," in Jelen, ed., *Sacred Markets*, 1–32.

17. See, for example, Steve Bruce, *God Is Dead: Secularization in the West* (Malden, Mass.: Blackwell, 2002); Pipa Norris and Ronald Inglehart, *Sacred and Secular: Religion and Politics Worldwide* (Cambridge, U.K.: Cambridge University Press, 2004).

18. Rodney Stark and Roger Finke, "To the Chinese Readers," *Xinyang de faze* (*Acts of Faith*) (Beijing: Renmin University Press, 2004), 3.

19. Thomas S. Kuhn, *The Structure of Scientific Revolutions* (Chicago: University of Chicago Press, 1962).

20. Peter L. Berger, "The Desecularization of the World: A Global Overview," in Peter L. Berger et al., eds., *The Desecularization of the World: Resurgent Religion and World Politics* (Eerdmans, 1999), 1–18.

21. Peter Berger, Grace Davie, and Effie Fokas, *Religious America, Secular Europe?: A Theme and Variations* (Aldershot, U.K.: Ashgate, 2008).

22. An example of this attitude is presented by Lizhu Fan, "The Dilemma of Chinese Religious Studies in the Framework of

Western Religious Theories," in Fenggang Yang and Graeme Lang, eds., *Social Scientific Studies of Religion in China: Methodology, Theories, and Findings* (Leiden: Brill, 2011), 87–108.

23. Grace Davie, *Religion in Britain since 1945: Believing without Belonging* (Oxford: Wiley-Blackwell, 1994); *Religion in Modern Europe: A Memory Mutates* (New York: Oxford University Press, 2000).

24. Rodney Stark and Laurence R. Iannaccone, "A Supply-Side Reinterpretation of the 'Secularization' of Europe," *Journal for the Scientific Study of Religion* 33, no. 3 (1994): 230–252; Rodney Stark and Roger Finke, *Acts of Faith: Explaining the Human Side of Religion* (Berkeley: University of California Press, 2000).

25. Eva M. Hamberg and Thorleif Pettersson, "The Religious Market: Denominational Competition and Religious Partici-pation in Contemporary Sweden," *Journal for the Scientific Study of Religion* 33 (1994): 205–216.

26. Grace Davie, *The Sociology of Religion* (London: Sage, 2007). In a previous article, Davie seems more hesitant than firm: "a map of the Rockies (i.e., more rigorous versions of rational choice theory) has to be adapted for use in Europe—just like the map of Alps (secularization theory) for those who venture in the reverse direction." "The Evolution of the Sociology of Religion: Theme and Variations" in Michele Dillon, ed., *Handbook of the Sociology of Religion* (New York: Cambridge University Press, 2003), 61–75.

27. Anthony J. Gill, *Rendering unto Caesar: The Roman Catholic Church and the State in Latin America* (Chicago: University of Chicago Press, 1998); Froese, "Hungary for Religion"; Froese, "After Atheism"; Froese, "Forced Secularization in Soviet Russia"; Froese and Pfaff, "Replete and Desolate Markets"; Gautier, "Church Attendance."

28. Stark and Finke, *Acts of Faith*, 193.

29. Roger Finke, "The Consequences of Religious Competition: Supply-side Explanations for Religious Change," in Lawrence A. Young, ed., *Rational Choice Theory and Religion: Summary and Assessment* (New York: Routledge, 1997), 50.

30. Stark and Finke, *Acts of Faith*, 198.

31. Ibid., 199.

32. Finke and Stark, *The Churching of America*.

33. Stark and Iannaccone, "A Supply-Side Reinterpretation; Stark and Finke, *Acts of Faith*, chap. 9.

34. Steve Bruce, *Sociology: A Very Short Introduction* (New York: Oxford University Press, 2000); and Lori G. Beaman, "The Myth of Plurality, Diversity and Vigour: Constitutional Privilege of Protestantism in the United States and Canada," *Journal for the Scientific Study of Religion*, 42 (2003): 311–325.

35. Peter Beyer, "Constitutional Privilege and Constituting Pluralism: Religious Freedom in National, Global, and Legal Context," *Journal for the Scientific Study of Religion* 42, no. 3 (2003): 333–339.

36. Anthony J. Gill, "Lost in the Supermarket: Comments on Beaman, Religious Pluralism, and What It Means to Be Free," *Journal for the Scientific Study of Religion* 42, no. 3 (2003): 327–331.

37. Mark Chaves and David E. Cann, "Regulation, Pluralism, and Religious Market Structure," *Rationality & Society* 4, no. 3 (1992): 272–290.

38. Tonin Gjuraj, "A Stable Ecumenical Model? How Religion Might Become a Political Issue in Albania," *Eastern European Quarterly* 34, no. 1 (2000): 21–49.

39. Stark and Finke, *Acts of Faith*, 255.

40. For example, Roger Finke and Laurence R. Iannaccone, "Supply-Side Explanations for Religious Change," *Annals of the American Academy of Political and Social Science* 527 (May 1993): 27–39; Stark and Iannaccone, "A Supply-Side Reinterpretation"; Finke, "The Consequences of Religious Competition"; Froese, "Hungary for Religion."

41. Finke and Stark, *The Churching of America*; Stark and Finke, *Acts of Faith*.

42. Eva M. Hamberg and Thorleif Pettersson, "Religious Markets: Supply, Demand, and Rational Choices," in Jelen, ed., *Sacred Markets*, 99. Also see Christopher G. Ellison and Darren E. Sherkat, "The 'Semi-involuntary Institution' Revisited:

Regional Variations in Church Participation among Black Americans," *Social Forces* 73, no. 4 (1995): 1415–1437; Darren E. Sherkat and John Wilson, "Preferences, Constraints, and Choices in Religious Markets: An Examination of Religious Switching and Apostasy," *Social Forces* 73 (1995): 993–1029; Darren E. Sherkat, "Embedding Religious Choices: Integrating Preferences and Social Constraints into Rational Choice Theories of Religious Behavior," in Lawrence A. Young, ed., *Rational Choice Theory and Religion: Summary and Assessment* (New York: Routledge, 1997), 65–85.

43. Stark and Finke, *Acts of Faith*, chap. 8.
44. János Kornai, *The Socialist System: The Political Economy of Communism* (Princeton, N.J.: Princeton University Press, 1992), 233.
45. Although the CCP-ruled Chinese authorities have insisted on calling it a "*socialist* market economy," while the meaning of "socialist" is debatable, since 2004, the Chinese government has repeatedly appealed to American and European countries in the World Trade Organization to recognize China's economy as a *full market economy*.
46. Wei Lü, "*Jin ru 'hou duan quan shiqi' de zhongguo jingji*" ("Chinese Economy Entered the 'Post-Shortage Period'") *Cai Jing Wenti Yan Jiu* (*Research on Financial and Economic Issues*), no. 3 (2001).
47. Christopher Marsh, *Unparalleled Reform: China's Rise, Russia's Fall, and the Interdependence of Transition* (New York: Lexington, 2006), 113–114.
48. Darren E. Sherkat and Christopher G. Ellison, "Recent Developments and Current Controversies in the Sociology of Religion," *Annual Review of Sociology* 25 (1999): 363–394; Stark and Finke, *Acts of Faith*; Mark Chaves and Philip S. Gorski, "Religious Pluralism and Religious Participation," *Annual Review of Sociology* 27 (2001): 261–281; Jelen, ed., *Sacred Markets*; David Voas, Daniel V. A. Olson, and Alasdair Crockett, "Religious Pluralism and Participation: Why Previous Research Is Wrong," *American Sociological Review* 67 (2002): 212–230; James Montgomery, "A Formalization and Test of the Religious

Economies Model," *American Sociological Review* 68 (2003): 782–809.

Chapter 2

1. For example, see Ronald L. Johnstone, *Religion in Society: A Sociology of Religion*, 8th ed. (Upper Saddle River, N.J.: Pearson Prentice Hall, 2007), 7–15; Meredith B. McGuire, *Religion: The Social Context*, 5th ed. (Belmont, Calif.: Wadsworth Thomson Learning, 2002), 8–15.

2. For example, Beatrice Leung, "China and Falun Gong: Party and Society Relations in the Modern Era," *Journal of Contemporary China* 11, no. 33 (2002): 761–784; Yunfeng Lu, "Entrepreneurial Logics and the Evolution of Falun Gong," *Journal for the Scientific Study of Religion* 44, no. 2 (2005): 173–185; and a special issue of *Nova Religio* on Falun Gong, 6 (2003).

3. James A. Beckford, *Social Theory and Religion* (Cambridge, U.K.: Cambridge University Press, 2003).

4. Peter Beyer, "Conceptions of Religion: On Distinguishing Scientific, Theological, and 'Official' Meanings," *Social Compass* 50 (2003): 141–160.

5. For example, Thomas A. Idinopulos and Brian C. Wilson, *What Is Religion? Origins, Definitions, and Explanations* (Leiden: Brill, 1998); André Droogers, "Defining Religion: A Social Science Approach," in Peter Clarke, ed., *The Oxford Handbook of the Sociology of Religion* (New York: Oxford University Press, 2009).

6. Max Weber, *The Sociology of Religion* (Boston: Beacon, 1963), 1.

7. For a comprehensive examination of this question, see Anna Sun, *Confusions over Confucianism: Controversies over the Religious Nature of Confucianism, 1870–2007*, dissertation, Princeton University, Princeton, N.J., 2009.

8. For example, Robert H. Nelson, *Economics as Religion: From Samuelson to Chicago and Beyond* (University Park, Pa.: Pennsylvania State University Press, 2002); Francis Ching-Wah Yip, *Capitalism as Religion? A Study of Paul Tillich's Interpretation of Modernity* (Harvard Theological Studies,

Harvard Divinity School, 2010); Joseph L. Price, *From Season to Season: Sports as American Religion* (Macon, Ga.: Mercer University Press, 2004); Emilio Gentile, *Politics as Religion*, trans. by George Staunton (Princeton, N.J.: Princeton University Press, 2006); John C. Lyden, *Film as Religion: Myth, Morals and Rituals* (New York: New York University Press, 2003).

9. A recent example is Mayfair Mei-Hui Yang, *Chinese Religiosities: Afflictions of Modernity and State Formation* (Berkeley and Los Angeles: University of California Press, 2008), especially 11.

10. Wilfred Cantwell Smith, *The Meaning and End of Religion* (New York: Macmillan, 1962), 20–21; Peter Beyer, "Social Forms of Religion and Religions in Contemporary Global Society," in Michele Dillon, ed., *Handbook of the Sociology of Religion* (New York: Cambridge University Press, 2003), 47; Yang, *Chinese Religiosities*, 13.

11. McGuire, *Religion*, 8.

12. William James, *The Varieties of Religious Experience* (New York: Modern Library, 1902), 42.

13. See Berger, *The Sacred Canopy;* McGuire, *Religion*, 10–15; J. Milton Yinger, *The Scientific Study of Religion* (New York: Macmillan, 1970), 4–5.

14. E. B. Tylor, *Primitive Culture* (London: Murray, 1871).

15. Emile Durkheim, *The Elementary Forms of Religious Life* (New York: Oxford University Press, 2001), 46.

16. Ibid., 32.

17. See Marco Orrù and Amy Wang, "Durkheim, Religion and Buddhism," *Journal for the Scientific Study of Religion* 31 (1992): 47–61.

18. Clifford Geertz, "Religion as a Cultural System," in M. Banton, ed., *Anthropological Approaches to the Study of Religion* (New York: Praeger, 1966), 4.

19. McGuire, *Religion*, 12.

20. Durkheim, *The Elementary Forms*, 42–43.

21. Ibid., 3.

22. Ibid., 6–7.

23. Ibid., 43.

24. Vincent Goossaert and David A. Palmer, *The Religious Question in Modern China* (Chicago and London: University of Chicago Press, 2011).

25. Yinger, *The Scientific Study of Religion*, 10.

26. Julia Corbett Hemeyer, *Religion in America*, 5th ed. (Upper Saddle River, N.J.: Pearson Prentice Hall, 2006), 17.

27. Weber, *The Sociology of Religion*, chap. 1.

28. Durkheim, *The Elementary Forms*, 41, 42.

29. Ibid., 43.

30. Johnstone, *Religion in Society*, 17.

31. Kenneth Dean, "Local Communal Religion in Contemporary South-East China," *China Quarterly* 174, no. 2 (2003): 338–358.

32. Yang, *Religion in Chinese Society*.

Chapter 3

1. The information in this and the following paragraphs is primarily derived from Gong Xuezeng, "A Sketch of the Studies of Marxist View of Religion in New China (Preface)," in Lü Daji and Gong Xuezeng, eds., *Marxist Approaches to Religions and Issues in Contemporary Chinese Religions* (Beijing: Minzu, 2008), 1–23.

2. This article does not make a distinction between religion and superstition, while the later, more nuanced political position asserts that religion and superstition are different without ever making clear articulations.

3. Dai Kangsheng, *"Xin zhongguo zongjiao yanjiu 50 nian"* ("50 Years of Religious Research in New China"), in Cao Zhongjian, ed., *Annual of Religious Research, 1999–2000* (Beijing: Religious Culture, 2001), 41.

4. Ibid., 43.

5. For a translation of and commentary of this CCP circular, see Donald E. MacInnis, *Religion in China Today: Policy and Practice* (Maryknoll, N.Y.: Orbis, 1994).

6. See He Guanghu, *"Zhongguo zongjiaoxue lilun yanjiu huigu"* ("Theoretical Development of Religious Research in China"), in Cao Zhongjian, ed., *Annual of Religious Research in China,*

1997–1998, (Beijing: Religious Culture Press, 2000), 79–91; Gao Shining, *"Zongjiaoxue jichu lilun yanjiu licheng"* ("Historical Development of the Basic Theoretical Research in Religious Studies"), in Cao, ed., *Annual of Religious Research in China, 1997–1998*, 73–78; and Dai, *"Xin zhongguo zongjiao yanjiu 50 nian"*. The best review I have seen is Duan Dezhi, *"Guanyu 'zongjiao yapian lun' de 'nan bei zhanzheng' jiqi xueshu gongxian"* ("Regarding the North-South Opium War of Religion and Its Academic Contribution"), *Fudan Journal*, no. 5 (2008), online at http://www.tecn.cn/data/21038.html.

7. Lü Daji, ed., *Zongjiaoxue tonglun (A General Essay on Religious Studies)* (Beijing: China Social Sciences, 1989), 80–81.

8. Lü Daji, *"Zongjiao shi shenme?—Zongjiao de benzhi, jiben yaosu, jiqi luoji jiegou"* ("What Is Religion?—The Essence, Elements, and Logical Structure of Religion"), in Cao Zhongjian, ed., *Annual of Religious Research, 1996* (Beijing: China Social Sciences, 1998), 81.

9. For example, Ge Zhaoguang, *Daoism and Chinese Culture* (Shanghai: Shanghai People's Press, 1987); Fang Litian, *Chinese Buddhism and Traditional Culture* (Shanghai: Shanghai People's Press, 1988); Zhuo Xinping, *Religion and Culture* (Beijing: People's Press, 1988).

10. Including such titles as *Aspects of Buddhist Culture, Aspects of Christian Culture*, and *Aspects of Islamic Culture*.

11. Including such titles as *A Hundred Questions of Christian Culture, A Hundred Questions of Buddhist Culture*, and *A Hundred of Questions of Islamic Culture*.

12. Interestingly, it is under the direct control of the State Religious Affairs Bureau. More interestingly, it has published Christian apologetics and Buddhist sutras.

13. Quoted in He, *"Zhongguo zongjiaoxue lilun yanjiu huigu,"* 85.

14. See Ka-che Yip, *Religion, Nationalism, and Chinese Students: The Anti-Christian Movement of 1922–1927* (Bellingham, Wash.: Center for East Asian Studies, Western Washington University, 1980); Jessie G. Lutz, *Chinese Politics and Christian Missions: The Anti-Christian Movements of 1920–28* (Notre Dame, Ind.: Cross Roads, 1988).

15. See Institute for the Study of Christian Culture in Chinese (ISCCC). *Wenhua jidutu: Xianxiang yu lunzheng (Cultural Christians: The Phenomenon and the Debate)* (Hong Kong: ISCCC, 1997); Cunfu Chen and Edwin Hsu, "*Wenhua jidutu xianxiang de zonglan yu fansi*" ("An Overview and Reflection on the Phenomenon of Cultural Christians"), *Regent Journal* (1998): 2–3; An Ximeng, "*Wenhua jidutu shi shenme ren?*" ("What Are the Cultural Christians?"), *Shijie Zongjiao Wenhua (World Religious Culture)* 1 (2000): 36–37; Zhuo Xinping, "Discussion on Cultural Christians in China," in S. Uhalley Jr. and Xiaoxin Wu, eds., *China and Christianity: Burdened Past, Hopeful Future* (Armonk, N.Y.: M. E. Sharpe, 2000), 283–300.

16. See Institute for the Study of Christian Culture in Chinese, *Cultural Christians.*

17. Ye Xiaowen published an article in 1997, "*Dangqian woguo de zongjiao wenti—Guanyu zongjiao wuxing de zai tantao*" ("Current Issues of Religion in Our Country—A Reexamination of the Five Characteristics of Religion"), which is included in Cao Zhongjian, ed., *Annual of Religious Research in China, 1997–1998* (Beijing: Religious Culture, 2000), 1–27.

18. Gong Xuezeng, *Shehuizhuyi yu zongjiao (Socialism and Religion)* (Beijing: Religious Culture, 2003).

19. Gong Xuezeng, "Comprehensive Grasping and Scientific Evaluating Leninist View of Religion," in Lü Daji and Gong Xuezeng, eds., *Marxist Approaches to Religions and Issues in Contemporary Chinese Religions* (Beijing: Minzu, 2008), 88–113.

20. Gong Xuezeng, *Zongjiao wenti gailun (General Introduction to Religious Problems)*, 3rd ed. (Chengdu: Sichuan Renmin, 2007), 2.

21. This article was published at *China Ethnic News*, January 16, 2007, p. 6.

22. Luo Zhufeng, ed., *Zhongguo shehuizhuyi shiqi de zongjiao wenti (Religious Problems in the Socialist Era of China)* (Shanghai: Shanghai Social Sciences, 1987). An English translation by Donald E. MacInnis was published as *Religion under Socialism in China* (Armonk, N.Y.: M.E. Sharpe, 1991).

23. See Wei Dedong, "*Zongjiao yu shehuizhuyi shehui xiang shi-ying lilun yanjiu huigu*" ("A Review of the Theoretical Research on the Compatibility of Religion and Socialist Society"), in Cao, ed., *Annual of Religious Research in China, 1997–1998*, 66–72; and Peter Tze Ming Ng, "From Ideological Marxism to Moderate Pragmatism: Religious Policy in China in the Turn of the Century," *China Review* (2000): 405–422.

Chapter 4

1. The Chinese Communist Party and the state of the People's Republic of China are not separable in most cases, even though specific policies and regulations may be announced by either the Party or the state or both. Therefore, I will use "Party-state" throughout this chapter except where the distinction needs to be differentiated.
2. In English, this religion has also been referred to as I-Kuan Tao, "the pervasive truth," "the consistent path," etc.
3. See Vincent Goossaert and David A. Palmer, *The Religious Question in Modern China* (Chicago and London: University of Chicago Press, 2011).
4. Luo Guangwu, *1949–1999 Xin zhongguo zongjiao gongzuo dashi gailan (A Brief Overview of Major Events of Religious Affairs in New China 1949–1999)* (Beijing: Huawen, 2001).
5. Ibid., 183.
6. Ibid., 223.
7. Ibid., 175–77.
8. Mass struggle meeting (*pi dou dahui*) was a form of public trial at a mass meeting, where the accused were exposed and criticized by the participating masses and often humiliated and tortured.
9. Luo, *1949–1999*, 164.
10. H. Welch, "Buddhism under the Communists," *China Quarterly* 6 (April–June 1961): 13; Donald W. Treadgold, *The West in Russia and China*, Vol. 2: *China, 1582–1949* (Cambridge, U.K.: Cambridge University Press, 1973), 69; Julian F. Pas, ed., *The Turning of the Tide: Religion in China Today* (Hong Kong, Oxford, and New York: Oxford University

Press, 1989), 20; Tony Lambert, *The Resurrection of the Chinese Church* (Wheaton, Ill.: Harold Shaw, 1994), 9.

11. Jiping Zuo, "Political Religion: The Case of the Cultural Revolution in China," *Sociological Analysis* 52, no. 1 (1991): 99–110.

12. See Pitman B. Potter, "Belief in Control: Regulation of Religion in China," *China Quarterly* 174, no. 2 (2003): 317–337.

13. Daodejing, also spelled Tao Te Ching, is considered the central scripture of Daoism.

14. For a translation of and commentary on this CCP circular, see MacInnis, *Religion in China Today*.

15. For example, Human Rights Watch/Asia, *Continuing Religious Repression in China* (New York: Human Rights Watch, 1993), and *China: State Control of Religion* (New York: Human Rights Watch, 1997); Center for Religious Freedom, *Report Analyzing Seven Secret Chinese Government Documents* (Washington, D.C.: Freedom House, 2002); Freedom House, "Freedom in the World—China (2007)," (http://www.freedomhouse.org/template.cfm?page=22&country=7155&year=2007); Potter, "Belief in Control"; Jason Kindopp and Carol Lee Hamrin, *God and Caesar in China: Policy Implications of Church-State Tensions* (Washington, D.C.: Brookings Institution, 2004); Eric R. Carlson, "China's New Regulations on Religion: A Small Step, Not a Great Leap, Forward," *Brigham Young University Law Review* 3 (2005): 747–797; Fuk-Tsang Ying, "New Wine in Old Wineskins: An Appraisal of Religious Legislation in China and the Regulations on Religious Affairs of 2005," *Religion, State & Society* 34, no. 4 (2006): 347–373.

Chapter 5

1. Jianbo Huang and Fenggang Yang, "The Cross Faces the Loudspeakers: A Village Church Perseveres under State Power," in Fenggang Yang and Joseph Tamney, eds., *State, Market, and Religions in Chinese Societies* (Leiden and Boston: Brill, 2005), 41–62.

2. Fenggang Yang and Dedong Wei, "The Bailin Buddhist Temple: Thriving under Communism," in Yang and Tamney, eds., *State, Market, and Religions*, 63–87.

3. Rodney Stark and William Simms Bainbridge, *The Future of Religion: Secularization, Revival, and Cult Formation* (Berkeley and Los Angeles: University of California Press, 1985); Arthur L. Greil and Thomas Robbins, eds., *Between Sacred and Secular: Research and Theory on Quasi-Religion* (Greenwich, Conn.: JAI, 1994); Wade Clark Roof, *Spiritual Marketplace: Baby Boomers and the Remaking of American Religion* (Princeton, N.J.: Princeton University Press, 1999); Paul Heelas and Linda Woodhead, *The Spiritual Revolution: Why Religion Is Giving Way to Spirituality* (Oxford and Malden, Mass.: Blackwell, 2005).

4. Stephen Sharot, *A Comparative Sociology of World Religions: Virtuosos, Priests, and Popular Religion* (New York: New York University Press, 2001); Max Weber, "The Social Psychology of the World Religions," in H. H. Gerth and C. Wright Mills, eds., *From Max Weber: Essays in Sociology* (London: Routledge and Kegan Paul, 1948), 267–301.

5. Zuo, "Political Religion."

6. Huang and Yang, "The Cross Faces the Loudspeakers; Yang and Wei, "The Bailin Buddhist Temple."

7. Greeley, "A Religious Revival in Russia?"; Mary L. Gautier, "Church Attendance and Religious Belief"; Froese, "Hungary for Religion"; Froese, "After Atheism"; Froese, "Forced Secularization"; Froese and Pfaff, "Replete and Desolate Markets."

8. John Anderson, *Religion, State and Politics in the Soviet Union and Successor States* (Cambridge, U.K.: Cambridge University Press, 1994); Olga Tchepournaya, "The Hidden Sphere of Religious Searches in the Soviet Union: Independent Religious Communities in Leningrad from the 1960s to the 1970s," *Sociology of Religion* 64, no. 3 (2003): 377–388.

9. Moshe Lewin, "Popular Religion in Twentieth-Century Russia," in Moshe Lewin, ed., *The Making of the Soviet System: Essays in the Social History of Interwar Russia* (New York: Pantheon, 1985), 57–71; Marjorie Mandelstam Balzer, ed., *Shamanism: Soviet Studies of Traditional Religion in Siberia and Central Asia*

(New York: M. E. Sharpe, 1990); Nina Tumarkin, *Lenin Lives! The Lenin Cult in Soviet Russia* (Cambridge, Mass.: Harvard University Press, 1983).

10. Zuo, "Political Religion."

11. Ye Xiaowen gave this speech in 1997 at the Central Party School. Ye, "Dangqian woguo de zongjiao wenti," 9.

12. Xinhua News Agency, "The Great Practice of the Freedom of Religious Belief: A Summary of the 60 Year's Religious Affairs since the Establishment of New China," September 4, 2009, http://news.xinhuanet.com/politics/2009-09/04/content _11997424.htm.

13. Daniel H. Bays, "Chinese Protestant Christianity Today," *China Quarterly* 174, no. 2 (2003): 492.

14. John Pomfret, "Evangelicals on the Rise in Land of Mao Despite Crackdowns, Protestant Religious Groups Flourishing in China," *Washington Post*, December 24, 2002, A01.

15. Richard Madsen, "Catholic Revival during the Reform Era," *China Quarterly* 174, no. 2 (2003): 471.

16. Luo, *1949–1999*.

17. In the late 1970s, many Catholic priests were released from prison, but Gong Pinmei was kept until being exiled to the United States for medical treatment in 1988.

18. Madsen, "Catholic Revival," 472.

19. Ibid., 473.

20. Ibid., 468.

21. Ibid., 472.

22. David Aikman, *Jesus in Beijing: How Christianity Is Transforming China and Changing the Global Balance of Power* (Washington, D.C.: Regnery, 2003); Jonathan Chao and Rosanna Chong, *A History of Christianity in Socialist China, 1949–1997* (Taipei: China Ministries International, 1997).

23. Madsen, "Catholic Revival," 492; see also Ryan Dunch, "Protestant Christianity in China Today: Fragile, Fragmented, Flourishing," in Stephen Uhalley Jr. and Xiaoxin Wu, eds., *China and Christianity: Burdened Past, Hopeful Future* (New York: M. E. Sharpe, 2001), 195–216.

24. Bays, "Chinese Protestant Christianity Today," 467–497.

25. Thomas David DuBois, *The Sacred Village: Social Change and Religious Life in Rural North China* (Honolulu: University of Hawaii Press, 2005).

26. Raoul Birnhaum, "Buddhist China at the Century's Turn," *China Quarterly* 174, no. 2 (2003): 428–450; Dru C. Gladney, "Islam in China: Accommodation or Separatism?" *China Quarterly* 174, no. 2 (2003): 451–467.

27. Gong Zhebing, "*Hubei Huanggang shi Daojiao de xianzhuang yu guanli*" ("The Status and Management of Daoism in Huanggang City, Hubei), *Journal of Religious Studies* 2 (2001): 52–58; Der-Ruey Yang, "The Changing Economy of Temple Daoism in Shanghai," in Yang and Tamney, eds., *State, Market, and Religions*, 115–150.

28. Madsen, "Catholic Revival," 483.

29. Shi Guoqing, *Zhuangzu Buluotuo xinyang yangjiu (A Study of the Buluotuo Beliefs of the Zhuang People)* (Beijing: Religious Culture, 2008); Lan Li, "The Changing Role of the Popular Religion of Nuo in Modern Chinese Politics," *Modern Asian Studies*, Cambridge Journals Online, 2010. DOI: 10.1017/S0026749X10000090.

30. Graeme Lang, Selina Ching Chan, and Lars Ragvald, *The Return of the Refugee God: Wong Tai Sin in China*, Chinese University of Hong Kong CSRCS, Occasional Paper No. 8, 2002, 14.

31. Yang, *Religion in Chinese Society*.

32. Kenneth Dean, *Lord of the Three in One* (Princeton, N.J.: Princeton University Press, 1998).

33. Kenneth Dean, *Taoist Ritual and Popular Cults of Southeast China* (Princeton, N.J.: Princeton University Press, 1993); Dean, *Lord of the Three in One*; Dean, "Local Communal Religion"; Khun Eng Kuah, *Rebuilding the Ancestral Village: Singaporeans in China* (Aldershot, U.K.: Ashgate, 2000); Jun Jing, *The Temple of Memories: History, Power, and Morality in a Chinese Village* (Stanford, Calif.: Stanford University Press, 1996); Zhentao Zhang, *The Cult of Houtu and the Music Associations in Hebei Province*, Chinese University of Hong Kong CSRCS, Occasional Paper No. 7, 2001; Lizhu Fan,

"The Cult of the Silkworm Mother as a Core of Local Community Religion in a North China Village: Field Study in Zhiwuying, Boading, Hebei," *China Quarterly* 174, no. 2 (2003): 359–372.

34. Jian Xu, "Body, Discourse, and the Cultural Politics of Contemporary Chinese Qigong," *Journal of Asian Studies* 58, no. 4 (1999): 961–992; Nancy N. Chen, *Breathing Spaces: Qigong, Psychiatry, and Healing in China* (New York: Columbia University Press, 2003); Nancy N. Chen, "Healing Sects and Anti-Cult Campaigns," *China Quarterly* 174, no. 2 (2003): 505–520; Congressional-Executive Commission on China, "Unofficial Religions in China: Beyond the Party's Rules," 2005, http://www.cecc.gov; David A. Palmer, *Qigong Fever: Body, Science, and Utopia in China* (New York: Columbia University Press, 2007).

35. Stark and Bainbridge, *The Future of Religion.*

36. A number of his articles initially published in official newspapers and magazines are collected in Yu Guangyuan, *Fan ren ti te yi gong neng lun (On Opposing Paranormal Powers)* (Guiyang: Guizhou Renmin, 1997).

37. Leung, "China and Falun Gong"; Lu, "Entrepreneurial Logics"; David Ownby, *Falun Gong and the Future of China* (Oxford: Oxford University Press, 2008).

38. Fenggang Yang, "Quantifying Religions in China," paper presented at the Seventh Conference of the Social Scientific Study of Religion in China, Beijing, July 26–27, 2010.

39. Liu Ping, *"Duo yuan qu xiang, chong shang ge xing, zi xin zi xing"* ("Pluralist Tendency, Individualistic Outlook, and Confidence and Reflectivity"), *Dangdai Qingnian Yanjiu (Research of Modern Young People)* 2 (1995): 1–5.

40. Adam Chau, *Miraculous Response: Doing Popular Religion in Contemporary China* (Stanford, Calif.: Stanford University Press, 2008).

41. Roger Finke, "Religious Deregulation: Origins and Consequences," *Journal of Church and State* 32(1990): 609–26.

42. Having seen state eradication measures during the Cultural Revolution, many scholars once pronounced the death of religion in China. See H. Welch, "Buddhism Under the

Communists," *China Quarterly* 6 (April-June 1961): 1–14, 13; Julian F. Pas, ed., *The Turning of the Tide: Religion in China Today* (Hong Kong, Oxford and New York: Oxford University Press, 1989): 20; Donald W. Treadgold, *The West in Russia and China*, Vol. II, *China 1582–1949* (Cambridge, MA: Cambridge University Press, 1973): 69; and Tony Lambert, *The Resurrection of the Chinese Church* (Wheaton, IL: Harold Shaw Publishers, 1994): 9.

Chapter 6

1. János Kornai, *Economics of Shortage* (Amsterdam, New York, and Oxford: North-Holland, 1980); Kornai, *The Socialist System.*
2. Kornai, *The Socialist System,* 245.
3. János Kornai, "Resource-Constrained versus Demand-Constrained Systems," *Econometrica* 47, no. 4 (1979): 802. Why individuals differ in response to shortage of supply or differ in religious preference is an interesting question, but that question is beyond the scope of this book.
4. Kornai, *The Socialist System,* 245.
5. Aikman, *Jesus in Beijing.*
6. Tony Lambert, *China's Christian Millions* (London and Grand Rapids, MI: Monarch Books, 1999); Aikman 2003; Jianbo Huang and Fenggang Yang, "The Cross Faces the Loudspeakers: A Village Church Perseveres Under State Power," in Fenggang Yang and Joseph Tamney, eds., *State, Market, and Religions in Chinese Societies* (Leiden, Netherlands and Boston, MA: Brill Academic Publishers, 2005).
7. European Values Study Group and World Values Survey Association, "European and World Values Surveys Integrated Data File, 1999–2002," Release 1 (computer file), 2nd Inter-university Consortium for Political and Social Research (ICPSR) version, 2004.
8. Quoted in Yang, *Religion in Chinese Society,* 5.
9. See ibid.; also see Küng and Ching, *Christianity and Chinese Religions.*
10. Yang, *Religion in Chinese Society,* 6.

11.   One other possibility for the low religiosity in the sample is that the Chinese sample was not representative of the population. Unfortunately, we do not have additional information about the sampling.

12.   Victor Yuan, "Chinese Beliefs and Spiritual Pursuits Today," in Fenggang Yang and Graeme Lang, eds., *Social Scientific Studies of Religion in China: Methodology, Theories, and Findings* (Leiden and Boston: Brill, 2011), 165–180.

13.   See Fenggang Yang and Joseph Tamney, eds., *Conversion to Christianity among the Chinese*, special issue, *Sociology of Religion* 67, no. 2 (2006).

14.   Paul Hollander, "Research on Marxist Societies: The Relationship between Theory and Practice," *Annual Review of Sociology* 8 (1982): 319–351.

15.   Timothy W. Luke, "Civil Religion and Secularization: Ideological Revitalization in Post-Revolutionary Communist Systems," *Sociological Forum* 2, no. 1 (1987): 114; emphasis in original.

16.   Ibid.; Zuo, "Political Religion"; Michael Burleigh, "National Socialism as a Political Religion," *Totalitarian Movements and Political Religions* 1, no. 2 (2000): 1–26.

17.   Richard Shorten, "The Enlightenment, Communism, and Political Religion: Reflections on a Misleading Trajectory," *Journal of Political Ideologies* 8, no. 1 (2003): 13–37.

18.   See Chinese Young Pioneers home page, http://cyc6.cycnet. com:8090/ccylmis/cypo/index.jsp.

19.   *Renmin Ribao (People's Daily)*, June 29, 2010, 1, 3.

20.   This is the latest public information, according to Xinhua News Agency, as of May 3, 2009; see http://www.ccyl.org.cn/ zhuanti/09_54/news/200905/t20090504_231106.htm.

21.   This is from the *Zhongguo Jiaoyu Bao (China Education Newspaper)*, June 2, 2010. For comparison, by the end of 2003, there were 68,232,000 CCP members and 3,341,000 grass-roots branches, 71,070,000 CCYL members and 2,983,000 grass-roots branches, and more than 130,000,000 CYP members in 350,000 brigades, according to Xinhua News Agency reports on May 3, May 31, and June 30, 2004.

22. According to the National Population and Family Planning Commission of P.R. China, the total population was 1,335,000,000 by the end of 2009; see http://www.chinapop.gov.cn/tjgb/201005/t20100526_204024.html.

23. Liu Ping, "*Duo yuan qu xiang.*"

24. Kornai, *The Socialist System,* 230–231.

25. Ibid., 230.

26. Jacob Heibrunn, "Mao More Than Ever," *New Republic* 216 (April 1997): 20–24; Bingzhong Gao and M. A. Qiang, "From Grass-Root Association to Civil Society: A Case Study of the Dragon Tablet Fair in Hebei Province," in Yang and Lang, eds., *Social Scientific Studies of Religion in China,* 195–226.

27. Zheng Wen, "*Dui kanxiang, suanming deng mixin huodong bu ke deng xian shi zhi*" ("Our Concerns about Physiognomy, Fortune-Telling and Other Superstitious Activities"), *Religions in China* (1997): 46–48.

28. *Kexue Shibao (Science Times),* "*Yiban yishang xianchuji gong-wuyuan nan ju 'mixin'*" ("More than Half of Public Service Officials at the County or Above Levels Have Difficulties to Resist 'Superstitions'"), May 11, 2007; see http://www.sciencetimes.com.cn/htmlnews/2007511193241656179151.html.

29. See *Chan* magazine, no. 3 (1991); http://chan.bailinsi.net/.

30. Li Qiaomei, "*Lun zhongguo dangdai zuojia de 'zongjiao re'*" ("On the 'Religious Fever' among Contemporary Writers of China"), *Guangdong Social Sciences* 4 (1996): 106–111; Michelle Yeh, "The 'Cult of Poetry' in Contemporary China," *Journal of Asian Studies* 55, no. 1 (1996): 51–31; Cai Rongan, "*Zongjiao re: Linghun de tong chu—dui jinnian lai meishu chuangzuo liu xiang de yi zhong kao lü*" ("Religious Fever: Pains of Souls—A Thought about a Trend of Art Creation in Recent Years"), *Jiangxi Normal University Journal* 2 (2002): 74–77; Yang, "Between Secularist Ideology and Desecularizing Reality."

31. Tony Lambert, *China's Christian Millions* (London and Grand Rapids, Mich.: Monarch, 1999), 24–25.

32. "A tourist is half a pilgrim, if a pilgrim is half a tourist." This mantra-like saying, attributed to Victor and Edith Turner, is quoted in William H. Swatos Jr., ed., *On the Road to Being*

There: Studies in Pilgrimage and Tourism in Late Modernity (Leiden and Boston: Brill, 2006), vii.

33. Lambert, *China's Christian Millions,* 156.
34. Laurence R. Iannaccone, "Why Strict Churches Are Strong," *American Journal of Sociology* 99 (1994): 1180–1211.
35. Kornai, *Economics of Shortage*; Kornai, *The Socialist System.*
36. Luo, *1949–1999,* 317.
37. Ibid., 436.
38. Ibid., 540.
39. See ibid.
40. According to the Chinese government's *White Paper: Freedom of Religious Belief in China,* in 1997, there were more than 85,000 sites for religious activity in the whole country. Some estimates put roughly 350,000 religious congregations in the United States. See C. Kirk Hadaway and Penny Long Marler, "How Many Americans Attend Worship Each Week? An Alternative Approach to Measurement," *Journal for the Scientific Study of Religion* 44, no. 3 (2005): 307–322. The U.S. population is less than 300 million, while the population in China is about 1.3 billion.
41. Republic of China Ministry of the Interior, *Bulletin of Statistics, Week 30 of 2010,* http://www.moi.gov.tw/stat/news_content.aspx?sn=4449&page=1.
42. Qi Wen, "*Shou ci zhongguo dangdai zongjiao xianzhuang yantaohui zai jing juxing*" ("The First Symposium on the Present Religious Situation in Contemporary China Was Held in Beijing"), *Research on World Religions* 1 (1991): 145–148; Luo Weihong, "*Shanghai zongjiao shinian fazhan chuyi*" ("A Preliminary Discussion of the Development of Shanghai Religion in the Past Ten Years"), *Contemporary Religious Research* 1 (1992): 23–29.
43. Xinhua News Agency, "The Great Practice of the Freedom of Religious Belief."
44. Luo, *1949–1999,* 392.
45. Ibid.
46. Christopher Marsh, "Revisiting China's 'Great Wall' of Separation: Religious Liberty in China Today," *Journal of Church and State* 50, no. 2 (Spring 2008): 210–211.

Chapter 7

1. Brian J. Grim and Roger Finke, *The Price of Freedom Denied: Religious Persecution and Conflict in the 21st Century* (New York: Cambridge University Press, 2010).
2. Jennifer Wynot, "Monasteries without Walls: Secret Monasticism in the Soviet Union, 1928–39," *Church History* 71 (March 2002): 63–79.
3. Anderson, *Religion, State and Politics*, 58. Also see Christopher Marsh, *Religion and the State in Russia and China: Suppression, Survival, and Revival* (New York: Continuum, 2011).
4. Lewin, "Popular Religion in Twentieth-Century Russia."; Balzer, ed., *Shamanism*.
5. Maryjane Osa, "Sacred Contention in the Great Novena," in Maryjane Osa, ed., *Solidarity and Contention: Networks of Polish Opposition* (Minneapolis: University of Minnesota Press, 2003), 59–80.
6. For example, Philip Clart, "Sects, Cults, and Popular Religion: Aspects of Religious Change in Post-War Taiwan," *British Columbia Asian Review* 9 (Winter 1995–96): 120–163; Philip Clart and Charles B. Jones, eds., *Religion in Modern Taiwan: Tradition and Innovation in a Changing Society* (Honolulu: University of Hawaii Press, 2003); Robert P. Weller, "Bandits, Beggars, and Ghosts: The Failure of State Control over Religious Interpretation in Taiwan," *American Ethnologist* 12, no. 1 (1985): 46–61.
7. Yunfeng Lu, *The Transformation of Yiguan Dao in Taiwan: Adapting to a Changing Religious Economy* (Lanham, Md.: Lexington, 2008).
8. For example, Peter B. Clarke, *Japanese New Religions in Global Perspective* (Richmond, U.K.: Curzon, 2000); Ichiro Hori, *Folk Religion in Japan: Continuity and Change* (Chicago: University of Chicago Press, 1994); Kim Sung-hae and James Heisig, eds., *Encounters: The New Religions of Korea and Christianity* (Seoul: Royal Asiatic Society, 2008); Yunshik Chang, Hyun-ho Seok, and Donald Baker, eds., *Korea Confronts Globalization* (New York: Routledge, 2009).

9. Fenggang Yang, "Hsi Nan Buddhist Temple: Seeking to Americanize," in Helen Rose Ebaugh and Janet S. Chafetz, eds., *Religion and the New Immigrants: Continuities and Adaptations in Immigrant Congregations* (Walnut Creek, Calif.: AltaMira, 2000), 67–87.

10. See, e.g., Berger, *The Sacred Canopy*; Warner, "Work in Progress"; Stark and Finke, *Acts of Faith*; Davie, *The Sociology of Religion*.

11. Speaking in economic terms, open-market competition without government interference may also result in oligopoly or monopoly of the market, but this chapter focuses on the oligopoly as a result of state regulations.

12. Anthony C. Yu, *State and Religion in China: Historical and Textual Perspectives* (Chicago and La Salle, Ill.: Open Court, 2005); Yoshiko Ashiwa and David Wank, eds., *Making Religion, Making the State: The Politics of Religion in Modern China* (Stanford, Calif.: Stanford University Press, 2009); Rebecca Nedostup, *Superstitious Regimes: Religion and the Politics of Chinese Modernity* (Cambridge, Mass.: Harvard University East Asian Monographs, 2010).

13. Gjuraj, "A Stable Ecumenical Model?"

14. Brian J. Grim and Roger Finke, "International Religion Indexes: Government Regulation, Government Favoritism, and Social Regulation of Religion," *Interdisciplinary Journal of Research on Religion* 2 (2006): Article 1.

15. Berger, *The Sacred Canopy*.

16. Warner, "Work in Progress"; Stark and Finke, *Acts of Faith*.

17. See Davie, *The Sociology of Religion*; Berger et al., eds., *The Desecularization of the World*.

18. Chaves and Gorski, "Religious Pluralism"; Voas, Olson, and Crockett, "Religious Pluralism and Participation"; James Montgomery, "A Formalization and Test"; Michael McBride, "Religious Pluralism and Religious Participation: A Game Theoretic Analysis," *American Journal of Sociology* 114, no. 1 (2008): 77–108.

19. James A. Beckford, "The Management of Religious Diversity in England and Wales with Special Reference to Prison Chaplaincy," *International Journal on Multicultural Societies* 1,

no. 2 (1999): 55–66, http://unesdoc.unesco.org/images/0014/001437/143733E.pdf#page=19.

20. Robert Wuthnow, "Presidential Address 2003: The Challenge of Diversity," *Journal for the Scientific Study of Religion* 43, no. 2 (2004): 162.

21. For example, David W. Machacek, "The Problem of Pluralism," *Sociology of Religion* 64, no. 2 (2003): 145–161; Peter Berger, "Concluding Remarks," Constituting the Future: A Symposium on Religious Liberty, Law, and Flourishing Societies, Istanbul, April 20–22, 2009.

22. Buster G. Smith, "Attitudes toward Religious Pluralism: Measurements and Consequences," *Social Compass* 54 (2007): 333–353.

23. Wuthnow, "Presidential Address," 162–163.

24. Pew Forum on Religion and Public Life, *Global Restrictions on Religion*, http://pewforum.org/newassets/images/reports/restrictions/restrictionsfullreport.pdf, 2009.

25. William V. D'Antonio and Dean R. Hoge, "The American Experience of Religious Disestablishment and Pluralism," *Social Compass* 53, no. 3 (2006): 346.

26. Ibid., 346–347.

27. Will Herberg, *Protestant-Catholic-Jew: An Essay in American Religious Sociology* (Garden City, N.Y.: Doubleday, 1955).

28. R. Stephen Warner and Judith Wittner, eds., *Gatherings in Diaspora: Religious Communities and the New Immigration* (Philadelphia: Temple University Press, 1998); Helen Rose Ebaugh and Janet S. Chafetz, eds., *Religion and the New Immigrants: Continuities and Adaptations in Immigrant Congregations* (Walnut Creek, Calif.: AltaMira, 2000); Dianna L. Eck, *A New Religious America: How a "Christian Country" Has Become the World's Most Religiously Diverse Nation* (San Francisco: Harper San Francisco, 2001).

29. Samuel Huntington, *Who Are We? The Challenges to American National Identity* (New York: Simon & Schuster, 2004).

30. For example, see Eck, *A New Religious America*; Dianna L. Eck, "AAR 2006 Presidential Address: Prospects for Pluralism: Voice and Vision in the Study of Religion," *Journal of the American Academy of Religion* 75, no. 4 (2007): 743–776.

31. For example, see Wuthnow, "Presidential Address"; Robert Wuthnow, *America and the Challenges of Religious Diversity* (Princeton, N.J.: Princeton University Press, 2007).
32. D'Antonio and Hoge, "The American Experience," 354.
33. Everett M. Rogers, *The Diffusion of Innovations*, 4th ed. (New York: Free Press, 1995).
34. Weber, *The Religion of China*; Yang, *Religion in Chinese Society*.
35. Stark and Finke, *Acts of Faith*.
36. Ibid., 198.
37. Ibid., 199.
38. Finke and Stark, *The Churching of America*.
39. Fenggang Yang, "Oligopoly Dynamics: Official Religions in China," in James Beckford and Jay Demerath III, eds., *The Sage Handbook of the Sociology of Religion* (London: Sage, 2007), 619–637.
40. Yang and Wei, "The Bailin Buddhist Temple."
41. For example, Chaves and Gorski, "Religious Pluralism."

BIBLIOGRAPHY

Aikman, David. *Jesus in Beijing: How Christianity Is Transforming China and Changing the Global Balance of Power.* Washington, D.C.: Regnery, 2003.

An, Ximeng. *"Wenhua jidutu shi shenme ren?"* ("What Are the Cultural Christians?"). *Shijie Zongjiao Wenhua (World Religious Culture)* 1 (2000): 36–37.

Anderson, John. *Religion, State and Politics in the Soviet Union and Successor States.* Cambridge, U.K.: Cambridge University Press, 1994.

Ashiwa, Yoshiko, and David Wank, eds. *Making Religion, Making the State: The Politics of Religion in Modern China.* Stanford, Calif.: Stanford University Press, 2009.

Balzer, Marjorie Mandelstam, ed. *Shamanism: Soviet Studies of Traditional Religion in Siberia and Central Asia.* Armonk, N.Y.: M. E. Sharpe, 1990.

Bays, Daniel H. "Chinese Protestant Christianity Today." *China Quarterly* 174, no. 2 (2003): 488–504.

Beaman, Lori G. "The Myth of Pluralism, Diversity and Vigor: The Constitutional Privilege of Protestantism In the United States and Canada." *Journal for the Scientific Study of Religion* 42, no. 3 (2003): 311–325.

Beckford, James A. "The Management of Religious Diversity in England and Wales with Special Reference to Prison Chaplaincy," *International Journal on Multicultural Societies* 1, no. 2 (1999): 55–66, http://unesdoc.unesco.org/images/0014/001437/143733E.pdf#page=19.

———. *Social Theory and Religion*. Cambridge, U.K.: Cambridge University Press, 2003.

Berger, Peter. "Concluding Remarks." Constituting the Future: A Symposium on Religious Liberty, Law, and Flourishing Societies, Istanbul, April 20–22, 2009.

———. "The Descularization of the World: A Global Overview." In Peter L. Berger et al., eds., *The Desecularization of the World: Resurgent Religion and World Politics*, 1–18. Grand Rapids, Mich.: Eerdmans, 1999.

———. *The Sacred Canopy: Elements of A Sociological Theory of Religion*. Garden City, N.Y.: Doubleday, 1967.

Berger, Peter, et al., eds. *The Desecularization of the World: Resurgent Religion and World Politics*. Grand Rapids, Mich.: Eerdmans, 1999.

Berger, Peter, Grace Davie, and Effie Fokas. *Religious America, Secular Europe?: A Theme and Variations*. Aldershot, U.K.: Ashgate, 2008.

Beyer, Peter. "Conceptions of Religion: On Distinguishing Scientific, Theological, and 'Official' Meanings." *Social Compass* 50 (2003): 141–160.

———. "Constitutional Privilege and Constituting Pluralism: Religious Freedom in National, Global, and Legal Context." *Journal for the Scientific Study of Religion* 42, no. 3 (2003): 333–340.

———. "Social Forms of Religion and Religions in Contemporary Global Society." In Michele Dillon, ed., *Handbook of the Sociology of Religion*, 45–60. New York: Cambridge University Press, 2003.

Birnhaum, Raoul. "Buddhist China at the Century's Turn." *China Quarterly* 174, no. 2 (2003): 428–450.

Bruce, Steve. *God Is Dead: Secularization in the West*. Malden, Mass.: Blackwell, 2002.

———. "The Myth of Plurality, Diversity and Vigour: Constitutional Privilege of Protestantism in the United States and Canada." *Journal for the Scientific Study of Religion* 42 (2003): 311–325.

————. *Sociology: A Very Short Introduction*. New York: Oxford University Press, 2000.

Burleigh, Michael. "National Socialism as a Political Religion." *Totalitarian Movements and Political Religions* 1, no. 2 (2000): 1–26.

Cai, Rongan. *"Zongjiao re: Linghun de tong chu—dui jinnian lai meishu chuangzuo liu xiang de yi zhong kao lü"* ("Religious Fever: Pains of Souls—A Thought about a Trend of Art Creation in Recent Years"). *Jiangxi Normal University Journal* 2 (2002): 74–77.

Carlson, Eric R. "China's New Regulations on Religion: A Small Step, Not a Great Leap, Forward." *Brigham Young University Law Review* 3 (2005): 747–797.

Carnes, Tony, and Fenggang Yang, eds. *Asian American Religions: The Making and Remaking of Borders and Boundaries*. New York: New York University Press, 2004.

Casanova, José. *Public Religions in the Modern World*. Chicago: University of Chicago Press, 1994.

Center for Religious Freedom. *Report Analyzing Seven Secret Chinese Government Documents*. Washington, D.C.: Freedom House, 2002.

Chang, Yunshik, Hyun-ho Seok, and Donald Baker, eds. *Korea Confronts Globalization*. New York: Routledge, 2009.

Chao, Jonathan, and Rosanna Chong. *A History of Christianity in Socialist China, 1949–1997*. Taipei: China Ministries International, 1997.

Chau, Adam. *Miraculous Response: Doing Popular Religion in Contemporary China*. Stanford, Calif.: Stanford University Press, 2008.

Chaves, Mark, and David E. Cann. "Regulation, Pluralism, and Religious Market Structure." *Rationality & Society* 4, no. 3 (1992): 272–290.

Chaves, Mark, and Philip S. Gorski. "Religious Pluralism and Religious Participation." *Annual Review of Sociology* 27 (2001): 261–281.

Chen, Cunfu, and Edwin Hsu. *"Wenhua jidutu xianxiang de zonglan yu fansi"* ("An Overview and Reflection on the Phenomenon of Cultural Christians"). *Regent Journal* 5, no. 1 (1998): 2–3.

Chen, Nancy N. *Breathing Spaces: Qigong, Psychiatry, and Healing in China.* New York: Columbia University Press, 2003.

———. "Healing Sects and Anti-Cult Campaigns." *China Quarterly* 174, no. 2 (2003): 505–520.

Chen, Susanna, ed. *Discerning Truth from Heresies: A Critical Analysis of the Alleged and Real Heresies in Mainland China.* Taipei: Christianity and China Research Center, 2000.

Clarke, Peter B. *Japanese New Religions in Global Perspective.* Richmond, U.K.: Curzon, 2000.

Clart, Philip. "Sects, Cults, and Popular Religion: Aspects of Religious Change in Post-War Taiwan." *British Columbia Asian Review* 9 (Winter 1995–96): 120–163.

Clart, Philip, and Charles B. Jones, eds. *Religion in Modern Taiwan: Tradition and Innovation in a Changing Society.* Honolulu: University of Hawaii Press, 2003.

Congressional-Executive Commission on China. "Unofficial Religions in China: Beyond the Party's Rules," 2005, http://www.cecc.gov.

Dai, Kangsheng. "*Xin zhongguo zongjiao yanjiu 50 nian*" ("50 Years of Religious Research in New China"). In Zhongjian Cao, ed., *Annual of Religious Research, 1999–2000*, 38–57. Beijing: Religious Culture, 2001.

D'Antonio, William V., and Dean R. Hoge. "The American Experience of Religious Disestablishment and Pluralism." *Social Compass* 53, no. 3 (2006): 345–356.

Davie, Grace. "The Evolution of the Sociology of Religion: Theme and Variations." In Michele Dillon, ed., *Handbook of the Sociology of Religion*, 61–75. New York: Cambridge University Press, 2003.

———. *Religion in Britain since 1945: Believing without Belonging.* Oxford: Wiley-Blackwell, 1994.

———. *Religion in Modern Europe: A Memory Mutates.* New York: Oxford University Press, 2000.

———. *The Sociology of Religion.* London: Sage, 2007.

Dean, Kenneth. "Local Communal Religion in Contemporary South-east China." *China Quarterly* 174, no. 2 (2003): 338–358.

———. *Lord of the Three in One.* Princeton, N.J.: Princeton University Press, 1998.

———. *Taoist Ritual and Popular Cults of Southeast China.* Princeton, N.J.: Princeton University Press, 1993.

Droogers, André. "Defining Religion: A Social Science Approach." In Peter Clarke, ed., *The Oxford Handbook of the Sociology of Religion,* 263–279. New York: Oxford University Press, 2009.

Duan, Dezhi. *"Guanyu 'zongjiao yapian lun' de 'nan bei zhanzheng' jiqi xueshu gongxian"* ("Regarding the North-South Opium War of Religion and Its Academic Contribution"). *Fudan Journal,* no. 5 (2008): 84–89.

DuBois, Thomas David. *The Sacred Village: Social Change and Religious Life in Rural North China.* Honolulu: University of Hawaii Press, 2005.

Dunch, Ryan. "Protestant Christianity in China Today: Fragile, Fragmented, Flourishing." In Stephen Uhalley Jr. and Xiaoxin Wu, eds., *China and Christianity: Burdened Past, Hopeful Future,* 195–216. Armonk, N.Y.: M. E. Sharpe, 2001.

Dunn, Emily Clare. *Heterodoxy and Contemporary Chinese Protestantism: The Case of Eastern Lightning,* PhD dissertation, University of Melbourne, 2010.

Durkheim, Emile. *The Elementary Forms of Religious Life.* New York: Oxford University Press, 2001.

Ebaugh, Helen Rose, and J. S. Chafetz, eds. *Religion and the New Immigrants: Continuities and Adaptations in Immigrant Congregations.* Walnut Creek, Calif.: AltaMira, 2000.

Eck, Dianna L. "AAR 2006 Presidential Address: Prospects for Pluralism: Voice and Vision in the Study of Religion." *Journal of the American Academy of Religion* 75, no. 4 (2007): 743–776.

———. *A New Religious America: How a "Christian Country" Has Become the World's Most Religiously Diverse Nation.* San Francisco: Harper San Francisco, 2001.

Ellison, Christopher G., and Darren E. Sherkat. "The 'Semi-involuntary Institution' Revisited: Regional Variations in Church Participation among Black Americans." *Social Forces* 73, no. 4 (1995): 1415–1437.

Fan, Lizhu. "The Cult of the Silkworm Mother as a Core of Local Community Religion in a North China Village: Field Study in Zhiwuying, Boading, Hebei." *China Quarterly* 174, no. 2 (2003): 359–372.

Fan, Lizhu. "The Dilemma of Chinese Religious Studies in the Framework of Western Religious Theories." In Fenggang Yang and Graeme Lang, eds., *Social Scientific Studies of Religion in China: Methodology, Theories, and Findings*, 87–108. Leiden and Boston: Brill, 2011.

Fang, Litian. *Chinese Buddhism and Traditional Culture*. Shanghai: Shanghai People's Press, 1988.

Finke, Roger. "The Consequences of Religious Competition: Supply-Side Explanations for Religious Change." In Lawrence A. Young, ed., *Rational Choice Theory and Religion: Summary and Assessment*, 45–64. New York: Routledge, 1997.

Finke, Roger, and Laurence R. Iannaccone. "Supply-Side Explanations for Religious Change." *Annals of the American Association for Political and Social Science* 527 (May 1993): 27–39.

Finke, Roger, and Rodney Stark. *The Churching of America, 1776– 1990: Winners and Losers in Our Religious Economy*. New Brunswick, N.J.: Rutgers University Press, 1992.

Freedom House. "Freedom in the World—China (2007)." http:// www.freedomhouse.org/template.cfm?page=22&country=71 55&year=2007.

———. "Report Analyzing Seven Secret Chinese Government Documents on Religious Freedom." Washington, D.C.: Hudson Institute.

Froese, Paul. "After Atheism: An Analysis of Religious Monopolies in the Post-Communist World." *Sociology of Religion* 65, no. 1 (2004): 57–75.

———. "Forced Secularization in Soviet Russia: Why an Atheistic Monopoly Failed." *Journal for the Scientific Study of Religion* 43, no. 1 (2004): 35–50.

———. "Hungary for Religion: A Supply-Side Interpretation of the Hungarian Religious Revival." *Journal for the Scientific Study of Religion* 40, no. 2 (2001): 251–268.

Froese, Paul, and Steven Pfaff. 2001. "Replete and Desolate Markets: Poland, East Germany, and the New Religious Paradigm." *Social Forces* 80, no. 2 (2001): 481–507.

Gao, Bingzhong, and M. A. Qiang. "From Grass-Root Association to Civil Society: A Case Study of the Dragon Tablet Fair in Hebei

Province." In Fenggang Yang and Graeme Lang, eds., *Social Scientific Studies of Religion in China: Methodology, Theories, and Findings*, 195–226. Leiden and Boston: Brill, 2011.

Gao, Shining. *"Zongjiaoxue jichu lilun yanjiu licheng"* ("Historical Development of the Basic Theoretical Research in Religious Studies"). In Cao Zhongjian, ed., *Annual of Religious Research in China, 1997–1998*, 73–78. Beijing: Religious Culture, 2000.

Gautier, Mary L. "Church Attendance and Religious Belief in Postcommunist Societies." *Journal for the Scientific Study of Religion* 36, no. 2 (1997): 289–297.

Ge, Zhaoguang. *Daoism and Chinese Culture*. Shanghai: Shanghai People's Press, 1987.

Geertz, Clifford. "Religion as a Cultural System." In M. Banton, ed., *Anthropological Approaches to the Study of Religion*, 1–46. New York: Praeger, 1966.

Gentile, Emilio. *Politics as Religion*, trans. by George Staunton. Princeton, N.J.: Princeton University Press, 2006.

Gill, Anthony. "Lost in the Supermarket: Comments on Beaman, Religious Pluralism, and What It Means to Be Free." *Journal for the Scientific Study of Religion* 42, no. 3 (2003): 327–332.

———. *Rendering unto Caesar: The Roman Catholic Church and the State in Latin America*. Chicago: University of Chicago Press, 1998.

Gjuraj, Tonin. "A Stable Ecumenical Model? How Religion Might Become a Political Issue in Albania." *East European Quarterly* 34, no. 1 (2000): 21–49.

Gladney, Dru C. "Islam in China: Accommodation or Separatism?" *China Quarterly* 174, no. 2 (2003): 451–467.

Gong, Xuezeng. "Comprehensive Grasping and Scientific Evaluating Leninist View of Religion." In Lü Daji and Gong Xuezeng, eds., *Marxist Approaches to Religions and Issues in Contemporary Chinese Religions*, 88–113. Beijing: Minzu, 2008.

———. *Shehuizhuyi yu zongjiao (Socialism and Religion)*. Beijing: Religious Culture, 2003.

———. "A Sketch of the Studies of Marxist View of Religion in New China (Preface)," In Lü Daji and Gong Xuezeng, eds., *Marxist Approaches to Religions and Issues in Contemporary Chinese Religions*, 1–23. Beijing: Minzu, 2008.

Gong, Xuezeng. *Zongjiao wenti gailun (General Introduction to Religious Problems)*, 3rd ed. Chengdu: Sichuan Renmin, 2007.

Gong, Zhebing. *"Hubei Huanggang shi Daojiao de xianzhuang yu guanli"* ("The Status and Management of Daoism in Huanggang City, Hubei"). *Journal of Religious Studies* 2 (2001): 52–58.

Goossaert, Vincent, and David A. Palmer. *The Religious Question in Modern China*. Chicago and London: University of Chicago Press, 2011.

Greeley, Andrew M. *Religious Change in America*. Cambridge, Mass.: Harvard University Press, 1989.

———. 1994. "A Religious Revival in Russia?" *Journal for the Scientific Study of Religion* 33, no. 3 (1994): 253–272.

Greil, Arthur L., and Thomas Robbins. *Between Sacred and Secular: Research and Theory on Quasi-Religion*. Greenwich, Conn.: JAI, 1994.

Grim, Brian J., and Roger Finke. "International Religion Indexes: Government Regulation, Government Favoritism, and Social Regulation of Religion." *Interdisciplinary Journal of Research on Religion* 2 (2006), Article 1 (online).

———. *The Price of Freedom Denied: Religious Persecution and Conflict in the 21st Century*. New York: Cambridge University Press, 2010.

Hadaway, C. Kirk, and Penny Long Marler. "How Many Americans Attend Worship Each Week? An Alternative Approach to Measurement." *Journal for the Scientific Study of Religion* 44, no. 3 (2005): 307–322.

Hamberg, Eva M., and Thorleif Pettersson. "The Religious Market: Denominational Competition and Religious Participation in Contemporary Sweden." *Journal for the Scientific Study of Religion* 33 (1994): 205–216.

———. "Religious Markets: Supply, Demand, and Rational Choices." In Ted G. Jelen, ed., *Sacred Markets, Sacred Canopies: Essays on Religious Markets and Religious Pluralism*, 91–114. Lanham, Md.: Rowman & Littlefield, 2002.

He, Guanghu. *"Zhongguo zongjiaoxue lilun yanjiu huigu"* ("Theoretical Development of Religious Research in China"). In Cao Zhongjian, ed., *Annual of Religious Research in China, 1997–1998*, 79–91. Beijing: Religious Culture, 2000.

Heelas, Paul, and Linda Woodhead. *The Spiritual Revolution: Why Religion Is Giving Way to Spirituality*. Oxford and Malden, Mass.: Blackwell, 2005.

Heibrunn, Jacob. "Mao More Than Ever." *New Republic* 216 (April 1997): 20–24.

Hemeyer, Julia Corbett. *Religion in America*, 5th ed. Upper Saddle River, N.J.: Pearson Prentice Hall, 2006.

Herberg, Will. *Protestant-Catholic-Jew: An Essay in American Religious Sociology*. Garden City, N.Y.: Doubleday, 1955.

Hoge, Dean R. *Converts, Dropouts, Returnees: A Study of Religious Change among Catholics*. New York: Pilgrim, 1981.

Hoge, Dean R., and David A. Roozen, eds. *Understanding Church Growth and Decline: 1950–1978*. New York: Pilgrim, 1979.

Hollander, Paul. "Research on Marxist Societies: The Relationship between Theory and Practice." *Annual Review of Sociology* 8 (1982): 319–351.

Hori, Ichiro. *Folk Religion in Japan: Continuity and Change*. Chicago: University of Chicago Press, 1994.

Huang, Jianbo, and Fenggang Yang. "The Cross Faces the Loudspeakers: A Village Church Perseveres under State Power." In Fenggang Yang and Joseph Tamney, eds., *State, Market, and Religions in Chinese Societies*. Leiden and Boston: Brill, 2005.

Human Rights Watch/Asia. *China: State Control of Religion*. New York: Human Rights Watch, 1997.

———. *Continuing Religious Repression in China*. New York: Human Rights Watch, 1993.

Hunter, Alan, and Kim-Kwong Chan. *Protestantism in Contemporary China*. Cambridge, U.K.: Cambridge University Press, 1993.

Huntington, Samuel. *Who Are We? The Challenges to American National Identity*. New York: Simon & Schuster, 2004.

Iannaccone, Laurence R. "Why Strict Churches Are Strong." *American Journal of Sociology* 99 (1994): 1180–1211.

Idinopulos, Thomas A., and Brian C. Wilson. *What Is Religion? Origins, Definitions, and Explanations*. Leiden. Brill, 1998.

Information Office of the PRC State Council. *White Paper on the Status of Human Rights in China*. Beijing: Information Office of the PRC State Council, 1991.

Institute for the Study of Christian Culture in Chinese (ISCCC). *Wenhua jidutu: Xianxiang yu lunzheng (Cultural Christians: The Phenomenon and the Debate)*. Hong Kong: ISCCC, 1997.

James, William. *The Varieties of Religious Experience*. New York: Modern Library, 1902.

Jelen, Ted G., ed. *Sacred Markets, Sacred Canopies: Essays on Religious Markets and Religious Pluralism*. Lanham, Md.: Rowman & Littlefield, 2003.

Jing, Jun. *The Temple of Memories: History, Power, and Morality in a Chinese Village*. Stanford, Calif.: Stanford University Press, 1996.

Johnstone, Ronald L. *Religion in Society: A Sociology of Religion*, 8th ed. Upper Saddle River, N.J.: Pearson Prentice Hall, 2007.

Kelly, Dean M. *Why Conservative Churches Are Growing*. New York: Harper & Row, 1972.

Kexue Shibao (Science Times). "*Yiban yishang xianchuji gongwuyuan nan ju 'mixin'*" ("More than Half of Public Service Officials at the County or Above Levels Have Difficulties to Resist 'Superstitions'"). May 11, 2007. See http://www.sciencetimes. com.cn/htmlnews/2007511193241656179151.html

Kim, Sung-hae, and James Heisig, eds. *Encounters: The New Religions of Korea and Christianity*. Seoul: Royal Asiatic Society, 2008.

Kindopp, Jason, and Carol Lee Hamrin. *God and Caesar in China: Policy Implications of Church-State Tensions*. Washington, D.C.: Brookings Institution, 2004.

Kornai, János. *Economics of Shortage*. Amsterdam, New York, and Oxford: North-Holland, 1980.

———. "Resource-Constrained versus Demand-Constrained Systems." *Econometrica* 47, no. 4 (1979): 801–820.

———. *The Socialist System: The Political Economy of Communism*. Princeton, N.J.: Princeton University Press, 1992.

Kuah, Khun Eng. *Rebuilding the Ancestral Village: Singaporeans in China*. Aldershot, U.K.: Ashgate, 2000.

Kuhn, Thomas S. *The Structure of Scientific Revolutions*. Chicago: University of Chicago Press, 1962.

Küng, Hans, and Julia Ching. *Christianity and Chinese Religions*. New York: Doubleday, 1989.

Lambert, Tony. *China's Christian Millions*. London and Grand Rapids, Mich.: Monarch, 1999.

———. *The Resurrection of the Chinese Church*. Wheaton, Ill.: Harold Shaw, 1994.

Lang, Graeme, Selina Ching Chan, and Lars Ragvald. *The Return of the Refugee God: Wong Tai Sin in China*. Chinese University of Hong Kong CSRCS, Occasional Paper No. 8, 2002.

Lechner, Frank J. "The 'New Paradigm' in the Sociology of Religion: Comment on Warner." *American Journal of Sociology* 103 (1997): 182–191.

Leung, Beatrice. "China and Falun Gong: Party and Society Relations in the Modern Era." *Journal of Contemporary China* 11, no. 33 (2002): 761–784.

Lewin, Moshe. "Popular Religion in Twentieth-Century Russia." In Moshe Lewin, ed., *The Making of the Soviet System: Essays in the Social History of Interwar Russia*, 57–71. New York: Pantheon, 1985.

Li, Lan. "The Changing Role of the Popular Religion of Nuo in Modern Chinese Politics." *Modern Asian Studies*, Cambridge Journals Online, 2010. DOI: 10.1017/S0026749X10000090.

Li, Pingye. "*90 Niandai zhongguo zongjiao fazhan zhuangkuang baogao*" ("A Report of the Status of Religious Development in China in the 1990s"). *Journal of Christian Culture* 2 (1999): 201–222.

Li, Qiaomei. "*Lun zhongguo dangdai zuojia de 'zongjiao re'*" ("On the 'Religious Fever' among Contemporary Writers of China"). *Guangdong Social Sciences* 4 (1996): 106–111.

Li, Shixiong, and Xiqiu Fu, eds. *China's Religious Freedom and "State Secrets" (PRC Classified Documents)*. New York: Committee for Investigation on Persecution of Religion in China, 2002.

Liu, Ping. 1995. "*Duo yuan qu xiang, chong shang ge xing, zi xin zi xing*" ("Pluralist Tendency, Individualistic Outlook, and Confidence and Reflectivity"). *Dangdai Qingnian Yanjiu (Research of Modern Young People)* 2 (1995): 1–5.

Lu, Yunfeng. "Entrepreneurial Logics and the Evolution of Falun Gong." *Journal for the Scientific Study of Religion* 44, no. 2 (2005): 173–185.

———. *The Transformation of Yiguan Dao in Taiwan: Adapting to a Changing Religious Economy*. Lanham, Md.: Lexington, 2008.

Lü, Daji. *"Zongjiao shi shenme?—Zongjiao de benzhi, jiben yaosu, jiqi luoji jiegou"* ("What Is Religion?—The Essence, Elements and Logical Structure of Religion"). In Cao Zhongjian, ed., *Annual of Religious Research, 1996,* 58–91. Beijing: China Social Sciences, 1998.

———, ed. *Zongjiaoxue tonglun (A General Essay on Religious Studies).* Beijing: China Social Sciences, 1989.

Lü, Wei. *"Jin ru 'hou duan quan shiqi' de zhongguo jingji"* ("Chinese Economy Entered the 'Post-Shortage Period'"). *Cai Jing Wenti Yanjiu (Research on Financial and Economic Issues),* no. 3 (2001).

Luke, Timothy W. "Civil Religion and Secularization: Ideological Revitalization in Post-Revolutionary Communist Systems." *Sociological Forum* 2, no. 1 (1987): 108–134.

Luo, Guangwu. *1949–1999 Xin zhongguo zongjiao gongzuo dashi gailan (A Brief Overview of Major Events of Religious Affairs in New China 1949–1999).* Beijing: Huawen, 2001.

Luo, Weihong. *"Shanghai zongjiao shinian fazhan chuyi"* ("A Preliminary Discussion of the Development of Shanghai Religion in the Past Ten Years"). *Contemporary Religious Research* 1 (1992): 23–29.

Luo Zhufeng. *Religion under Socialism in China,* trans. Donald E. MacInnis. Armonk, N.Y.: M. E. Sharpe, 1991.

———, ed. *Zhongguo shehuizhuyi shiqi de zongjiao wenti (Religious Problems in the Socialist Era of China).* Shanghai: Shanghai Social Sciences, 1987.

Lutz, Jessie G. *Chinese Politics and Christian Missions: The Anti-Christian Movements of 1920–28.* Notre Dame, Ind.: Cross Roads, 1988.

Lyden, John C. *Film as Religion: Myth, Morals and Rituals.* New York: New York University Press, 2003.

Machacek, David W. "The Problem of Pluralism." *Sociology of Religion* 64, no. 2 (2003): 145–161.

MacInnis, Donald E. *Religion in China Today: Policy and Practice.* Maryknoll, N.Y.: Orbis, 1989.

———. "The Secular Vision of a New Humanity in People's China." *Christian Century* (March 12, 1974): 249–253.

Madsen, Richard. "Catholic Revival during the Reform Era." *China Quarterly* 174, no. 2 (2003): 468–487.

————. *China's Catholics: Tragedy and Hope in an Emerging Civil Society.* Los Angeles and Berkeley: University of California Press, 1998.

Marsh, Christopher. *Religion and the State in Russia and China: Suppression, Survival, and Revival.* New York: Continuum, 2011.

————. "Revisiting China's 'Great Wall' of Separation: Religious Liberty in China Today." *Journal of Church and State* 50, no. 2 (Spring 2008): 210–211.

————. *Unparalled Reform: China's Rise, Russia's Fall, and the Interdependence of Transition.* New York: Lexington, 2006.

Martin, David. *On Secularization: Towards A Revised General Theory.* Aldershot, U.K.: Ashgate, 2005.

McBride, Michael. "Religious Pluralism and Religious Participation: A Game Theoretic Analysis." *American Journal of Sociology* 114, no. 1 (2008): 77–108.

McGuire, Meredith B. *Religion: The Social Context,* 5th ed. Belmont, Calif.: Wadsworth Thomson Learning, 2002.

Montgomery, James. "A Formalization and Test of the Religious Economies Model." *American Sociological Review* 68 (2003): 782–809.

Mou Zhongjian. "*Zhongguo shehuizhuyizhe yinggai shi wenhe wushenlunzhe*" ("The Chinese Socialists Ought to Be Mild Atheists"). *China Ethnic News,* January 16, 2007.

Musick, M., and J. Wilson. "Religious Switching for Marriage Reasons," *Sociology of Religion* 56 (1995): 257–270.

Nedostup, Rebecca. *Superstitious Regimes: Religion and the Politics of Chinese Modernity.* Cambridge, Mass.: Harvard University East Asian Monographs, 2010.

Nelson, Robert H. *Economics as Religion: From Samuelson to Chicago and Beyond.* University Park, Pa.: Pennsylvania State University Press, 2002.

Newport, F. "The Religious Switchers in the United States." *American Sociological Review* 44 (1979): 528–552.

Ng, Peter Tze Ming. "From Ideological Marxism to Moderate Pragmatism: Religious Policy in China in the Turn of the Century." *China Review* (2000): 405–422.

Norris, Pipa, and Ronald Inglehart. *Sacred and Secular: Religion and Politics Worldwide.* Cambridge, U.K.: Cambridge University Press, 2004.

Nova Religio 6 (2003). Special issue on Falun Gong.

Ownby, David. *Falun Gong and the Future of China.* Oxford: Oxford University Press, 2008.

Orrù, Marco, and Amy Wang. "Durkheim, Religion and Buddhism." *Journal for the Scientific Study of Religion* 31 (1992): 47–61.

Osa, Maryjane. "Sacred Contention in the Great Novena." In Maryjane Osa, ed., *Solidarity and Contention: Networks of Polish Opposition*, 59–80. Minneapolis: University of Minnesota Press, 2003.

Palmer, David A. *Qigong Fever: Body, Charisma, and Utopia in China.* New York: Columbia University Press, 2007.

Pas, Julian F., ed. *The Turning of the Tide: Religion in China Today.* Hong Kong, Oxford, and New York: Oxford University Press, 1989.

Pew Forum on Religion and Public Life. *Global Restrictions on Religion.* http://pewforum.org/newassets/images/reports/restrictions/restrictionsfullreport.pdf, 2009.

Pomfret, John. "Evangelicals on the Rise in Land of Mao Despite Crackdowns, Protestant Religious Groups Flourishing in China." *Washington Post*, December 24, 2002, A01.

Potter, Pitman B. "Belief in Control: Regulation of Religion in China." *China Quarterly* 174, no. 2 (2003): 317–337.

Price, Joseph L. *From Season to Season: Sports as American Religion.* Macon, Ga.: Mercer University Press, 2004.

Qi, Wen. "*Shou ci zhongguo dangdai zongjiao xianzhuang yantaohui zai jing juxing*" ("The First Symposium on the Present Religious Situation in Contemporary China Was Held in Beijing"). *Research on World Religions* 1 (1991): 145–148.

Rogers, Everett M. *The Diffusion of Innovations*, 4th ed. New York: Free Press, 1995.

Roof, Wade Clark. *Spiritual Marketplace: Baby Boomers and the Remaking of American Religion.* Princeton, N.J.: Princeton University Press, 1999.

Roof, W. C., and C. K. Hadaway. "Denominational Switching: Going beyond Stark and Glock," *Journal for the Scientific Study of Religion* 18 (1979): 363–379.

Roozen, D. A., and C. K. Hadaway, eds. *Church and Denominational Growth.* Nashville, Tenn.: Abingdon, 1993.

Sharot, Stephen. *Priests,and Popular Religion*. New York: New York University Press, 2001.

Sherkat, Darren E. "Embedding Religious Choices: Integrating Preferences and Social Constraints into Rational Choice Theories of Religious Behavior." In Lawrence A. Young, ed., *Rational Choice Theory and Religion: Summary and Assessment*, 65–85. New York: Routledge, 1997.

Sherkat, Darren E., and Christopher G. Ellison. "Recent Developments and Current Controversies in the Sociology of Religion." *Annual Review of Sociology* 25 (1999): 363–394.

Shi, Guoqing. *Zhuangzu Buluotuo xinyang yangjiu (A Study of the Buluotuo Beliefs of the Zhuang People)*. Beijing: Religious Culture, 2008.

Shorten, Richard. "The Enlightenment, Communism, and Political Religion: Reflections on a Misleading Trajectory." *Journal of Political Ideologies* 8, no. 1 (2003): 13–37.

Smith, Buster G. "Attitudes toward Religious Pluralism: Measurements and Consequences." *Social Compass* 54, no. 2 (2007): 333–353.

Smith, Wilfred Cantwell. *The Meaning and End of Religion*. New York: Macmillan, 1962.

Stark, Rodney. "Secularization, R.I.P.," *Sociology of Religion* 60 (1999): 249–273.

Stark, Rodney, and William Simms Bainbridge. *The Future of Religion: Secularization, Revival, and Cult Formation*. Berkeley and Los Angeles: University of California Press, 1985.

Stark, Rodney, and Roger Finke. *Acts of Faith: Explaining the Human Side of Religion*. Berkeley and Los Angeles: University of California Press, 2000.

———. "To the Chinese Readers." *Xinyang de faze (Acts of Faith)*. Beijing: Renmin University Press, 2004.

Stark, Rodney, and Laurence R. Iannaccone. "A Supply-Side Reinterpretation of the 'Secularization' of Europe." *Journal for the Scientific Study of Religion* 33, no. 3 (1994); 230–252.

Sun, Anna. *Confusions over Confucianism: Controversies over the Religious Nature of Confucianism, 1870–2007*. PhD dissertation, Princeton University, Princeton, N.J., 2009.

Swatos, William H. Jr., ed. *On the Road to Being There: Studies in Pilgrimage and Tourism in Late Modernity*. Leiden and Boston: Brill, 2006.

Tang Yao. *"Makesi liening zhuyi yu zongjiao wenti"* ("Marxism-Leninism on the Religious Problem"). *Zhexue Yanjiu (Journal of Philosophical Research)*, no. 5 (1956): 74–102.

Tchepournaya, Olga. "The Hidden Sphere of Religious Searches in the Soviet Union: Independent Religious Communities in Leningrad from the 1960s to the 1970s." *Sociology of Religion* 64, no. 3 (2003): 377–388.

Treadgold, Donald W. *The West in Russia and China*, Vol. 2: *China 1582–1949*. Cambridge, U.K.: Cambridge University Press, 1973.

Tumarkin, Nina. *Lenin Lives! The Lenin Cult in Soviet Russia*. Cambridge, Mass.: Harvard University Press, 1983.

Tylor, E. B. *Primitive Culture*. London: Murray, 1871.

Voas, David, Daniel Olson, and Alasdair Crockett. "Religious Pluralism and Participation: Why Previous Research Is Wrong." *American Sociological Review* 67 (2002): 212–230.

Warner, R. Stephen. "Equality and Exchange: The Sociological Research of Religion in Contemporary Contexts" (interview). *China Ethnic News*, September 19, 2008.

———. "Hoping Chinese Scholars to Develop Theories and the Paradigm More Suitable to Explain Religion in China" (interview). *China Ethnic News*, July 25, 2006.

———. "More Progress on the New Paradigm." In Ted G. Jelen, ed., *Sacred Markets, Sacred Canopies: Essays on Religious Markets and Religious Pluralism*, 1–32. Lanham, Md.: Rowman & Littlefield, 2003.

———. "A Paradigm Is Not a Theory: Reply to Lechner." *American Journal of Sociology* 103 (1997): 192–199.

———. "Work in Progress toward a New Paradigm for the Sociological Study of Religion in the United States." *American Journal of Sociology* 98 (1993): 1044–1093.

Warner, R. Stephen, and Judith Wittner, eds. *Gatherings in Diaspora: Religious Communities and the New Immigration*. Philadelphia: Temple University Press, 1998.

Weber, Max. *The Protestant Ethic and the Spirit of Capitalism*. New York: Scribner's, 1958.

————. *The Religion of China.* New York: Free Press, 1951 [1916–17].

————. "The Social Psychology of the World Religions." In H. H. Gerth and C. Wright Mills, eds., *From Max Weber: Essays in Sociology*, 267–301. London: Routledge and Kegan Paul, 1948.

————. *The Sociology of Religion.* Boston: Beacon, 1963.

Wei, Dedong. "*Zongjiao yu shehuizhuyi shehui xiang shiying lilun yanjiu huigu*" ("A Review of the Theoretical Research on the Compatibility of Religion and Socialist Society"). In Cao Zhongjian, ed., *Annual of Religious Research in China, 1997–1998*, 66–72. Beijing: Religious Culture, 2000.

Welch, H. "Buddhism under the Communists." *China Quarterly* 6 (April–June 1961): 1–14.

Weller, Robert P. "Bandits, Beggars, and Ghosts: The Failure of State Control over Religious Interpretation in Taiwan." *American Ethnologist* 12, no. 1 (1985): 46–61.

Wuthnow, Robert. *America and the Challenges of Religious Diversity.* Princeton, N.J.: Princeton University Press, 2007.

————. "Presidential Address 2003: The Challenge of Diversity." *Journal for the Scientific Study of Religion* 43, no. 2 (2004): 159–170.

Wynot, Jennifer. "Monasteries without Walls: Secret Monasticism in the Soviet Union, 1928–39." *Church History* 71 (March 2002): 63–79.

Xinhua News Agency. "The Great Practice of the Freedom of Religious Belief: A Summary of the 60 Year's Religious Affairs since the Establishment of New China." September 4, 2009; http://news.xinhuanet.com/politics/2009-09/04/content_11997424.htm.

Xu, Jian. "Body, Discourse, and the Cultural Politics of Contemporary Chinese Qigong." *Journal of Asian Studies* 58, no. 4 (1999): 961–992.

Yang, C. K. *Religion in Chinese Society.* Berkeley and Los Angeles: University of California Press, 1961.

Yang, Der Ruey. "The Changing Economy of Temple Daoism in Shanghai." In Fenggang Yang and Joseph B. Tamney, eds., *State, Market, and Religions in Chinese Societies*, 115–150. Leiden and Boston: Brill, 2005.

Yang, Fenggang. "The Change of the Notion of God in Western Philosophy." *Nankai Journal*, no. 1 (1988): 34–39.

———. *Chinese Christians in America: Conversion, Assimilation, and Adhesive Identities.* University Park, Pa.: Penn State University Press, 1999.

———. "Hsi Nan Buddhist Temple: Seeking to Americanize." In Helen Rose Ebaugh and Janet S. Chafetz, eds., *Religion and the New Immigrants: Continuities and Adaptations in Immigrant Congregations*, 67–87. Walnut Creek, Calif.: AltaMira, 2000.

———. "Between Secularist Ideology and Desecularizing Reality: The Birth and Growth of Religious Research in Communist China." *Sociology of Religion* 65, no. 2 (2004): 101–119.

———. "Lost in the Market, Saved at McDonald's: Conversion to Christianity in Urban China." *Journal for the Scientific Study of Religion* 44 (2005): 423–441.

———. "The Red, Black, and Gray Markets of Religion in China." *Sociological Quarterly* 47 (2006): 93–122.

———. "Oligopoly Dynamics: Consequences of Religious Regulation," Social Compass 57 (2010): 194–205.

———. "Oligopoly Dynamics: Official Religions in China." In James Beckford and Jay Demerath III, eds., *The Sage Handbook of the Sociology of Religion*, 619–637. London: Sage, 2007.

———. "Quantifying Religions in China." Paper presented at the Seventh Conference of the Social Scientific Study of Religion in China, Beijing, July 26–27, 2010.

Yang, Fenggang, and Helen Rose Ebaugh. "Religion and Ethnicity among New Immigrants: The Impact of Majority/Minority Status in Home and Host Countries." *Journal for the Scientific Study of Religion* 40 (2001): 367–378.

———. "Transformations in New Immigrant Religions and Their Global Implications." *American Sociological Review* 66 (2001): 269–88.

Yang, Fenggang, and Graeme Lang, eds. *Social Scientific Studies of Religion in China: Methodology, Theories, and Findings.* Leiden and Boston: Brill, 2011.

Yang, Fenggang, and Joseph Tamney, eds. *State, Market, and Religions in Chinese Societies.* Leiden and Boston: Brill, 2005.

————. *Conversion to Christianity among the Chinese.* Special issue of *Sociology of Religion* 67, no. 2 (2006).

Yang, Fenggang, and Dedong Wei. "The Bailin Buddhist Temple: Thriving under Communism." In Fenggang Yang and Joseph B. Tamney, eds., *State, Market, and Religions in Chinese Societies,* 63–86. Leiden and Boston: Brill, 2005.

Yang, Mayfair Mei-Hui. *Chinese Religiosities: Afflictions of Modernity and State Formation.* Berkeley and Los Angeles: University of California Press, 2008.

Ye, Xiaowen. "*Dangqian woguo de zongjiao wenti—Guanyu zongjiao wu xing de zai tantao*" ("Current Issues of Religion in Our Country—A Reexamination of the Five Characteristics of Religion"). In Cao Zhongjian, ed., *Annual of Religious Research in China, 1997–1998,* 1–27. Beijing: Religious Culture, 2000 [1997].

Yeh, Michelle. "The 'Cult of Poetry' in Contemporary China." *Journal of Asian Studies* 55, no. 1 (1996): 51–31.

Ying, Fuk-Tsang. "New Wine in Old Wineskins: An Appraisal of Religious Legislation in China and the Regulations on Religious Affairs of 2005." *Religion, State & Society* 34, no. 4 (2006): 347–373.

Yinger, J. Milton. *The Scientific Study of Religion.* New York: Macmillan, 1970.

Yip, Francis Ching-Wah. *Capitalism as Religion? A Study of Paul Tillich's Interpretation of Modernity.* Cambridge, Mass.: Harvard Divinity School, 2010.

Yip, Ka-che. *Religion, Nationalism, and Chinese Students: The Anti-Christian Movement of 1922–1927.* Bellingham, Wash.: Center for East Asian Studies, Western Washington University, 1980.

You Xiang and Liu Junwang. "*Makesi liening zhuyi zongjiaoguan de jige wenti*" ("Some Issues of the Marxist-Leninist View of Religion"). *Xinjianshe (New Construction)*, no. 9 (1963): n.p.

————. "*Zhengque renshi he chuli zongjiao wenti*" ("Correctly Knowing and Dealing with the Problem of Religion"). *Hongqi (Red Flag)*, no. 138 (February 26, 1964): 34–41.

Young, Lawrence, ed., *Rational Choice Theory and Religion: Summary and Assessment.* New York: Routledge, 1997.

Yu, Anthony C. *State and Religion in China: Historical and Textual Perspectives.* Chicago and La Salle, Ill.: Open Court, 2005.

Yu, Guangyuan. *Fan ren ti te yi gong neng lun (On Opposing Paranormal Powers)*. Guiyang: Guizhou Renmin, 1997.

Yuan, Victor. "Chinese Beliefs and Spiritual Pursuits Today." In Fenggang Yang and Graeme Lang, eds., *Social Scientific Studies of Religion in China: Methodology, Theories, and Findings*. Leiden and Boston: Brill, 2011.

Zhang, Zhentao. *The Cult of Houtu and the Music Associations in Hebei Province*. Chinese University of Hong Kong CSRCS, Occasional Paper No. 7, 2001.

Zheng, Wen. "*Dui kanxiang, suanming deng mixin huodong bu ke deng xian shi zhi*" ("Our Concerns about Physiognomy, Fortune-Telling and Other Superstitious Activities"). *Religions in China* (1997): 46–48.

Zhuo, Xinping. *Religion and Culture*. Beijing: People's Press, 1988.

Zuo, Jiping. "Political Religion: The Case of the Cultural Revolution in China." *Sociological Analysis* 52, no. 1 (1991): 99–110.

INDEX

supply-side explanations, 126
supply-side theory, 18–19, 23
suppression, of religious
demand, 128–33

Tamney, Joseph, 181n5
Tang Yao, 48
Tao Te Ching. *See* Daodejing
taxation, 16
temples
Buddhist, 145, 151
closures, 82
Daoist, 75, 151
government revival of, 110–11
Huang Daxian, 110
Mazu, 109–10
official statistics on, 94*t*
Shaolin, 128
village and ancestral, 112
theoreticians. *See* Marxist
theoreticians, opium war
among
theories
of religions, 32–34
secularization, 3–5
supply-side, 18–19, 23
Thought Liberation
campaigns, 54–55
Three-in-One cult, 112, 177
Three Ranks of
Servants, 104*t*
Three-Selfs principle, 68
Tiananmen massacre, 148

Tianhou, 110. *See also* Mazu
Tibet, 54, 70–71
Tibetan Buddhism, 106
Mao on, 70–71
reincarnation in, 98
Tito, Josip Broz, 139
topography, 12–13, 185n26
torture, 193n8
totemism, 41
tourism, 110–11
triple religious markets. *See
also* black-market religion;
gray-market religion;
red-market religion
dynamics of, 120–22
in other societies, 160–63
True Buddha sect, 106
True Orthodox, 161
truth
in facts, 4
pervasive, 193n2
Tudi (earth god), 112
Tulao people, 110
tutelage cults, 41
Tylor, E. B., 30, 36

underground. *See also* black-
market religion
activities of Roman Catholic
church, 100, 109
Buddhists, 106, 128
churches and growth
of, 102, 103*t*, 104*t*, 105*t*